CHS Humanities Dept.

D0966341

STORIES IN HISTORY

THE
RENAISSANCE

1300-1600

nextext

Cover illustration: Todd Leonardo

Printed in the United States of America

ISBN 0-618-14224-X

4 5 6 7 8 9 — QVK — 06 05 04 03

Table of Contents

from Giovanni Boccaccio's *Decameron*

Retold by Walter Hazen

*Ten young people have left Florence because of
the plague. They tell stories to pass the time and
calm their fears. Now it's Fiametta's turn. . . .*

About this Book

The stories are historical fiction. They are based on historical fact, but some of the characters and events may be fictional. In the Sources section you'll learn which is which and where the information came from.

The illustrations are all historical. If they are from a time different from the story, the caption tells you. Original documents help you understand the time period. Maps let you know where things were.

Items explained in People and Terms to Know are repeated in the Glossary. Look there if you come across a name or term you don't know.

Historians do not always agree on the exact dates of events in the ancient past. The letter c before a date means "about" (from the Latin word circa).

If you would like to read more about these exciting times, you will find recommendations in Reading on Your Own.

Background

How beauteous mankind is! O brave new world
That has such people in't!

—Miranda, in Shakespeare's *The Tempest* (1611)

A New Age Begins

Men can do all things if they will.
                    —Leon Battista Alberti (1404–1472)

In the 1300s, some new ideas sparked minds in northern Italy. A blaze of creativity followed that swept throughout much of Europe. Historians call this period the Renaissance, which means "rebirth." What was reborn was a belief that there were no limits to what human beings could accomplish.

Learning from the Ancients

During the Middle Ages, the Church had preserved much ancient learning from Greece and Rome. But this learning lay buried in writings that few people read. In the 1300s, this began to change. People rediscovered the ancient writings. What they found was evidence of a great classical civilization. They read poetry, history, philosophy, drama, science, and writings about art and architecture. They saw the great things that human beings had once accomplished. They began to dream about what they might achieve.

Humanism and the Arts

The study of ancient Greece and Rome led to a new outlook on life called humanism. The people who adopted this new outlook were called humanists. Humanism challenged the tradition of the Middle Ages in important ways. First, humanists replaced

▲
This Renaissance painting uses the technique of perspective to make the scene look three-dimensional.

the interest in spiritual life with an interest in this world. Second, humanists celebrated human freedom. They believed that human beings could accomplish anything.

The humanists believed that a person could enjoy life without offending God. This new attitude changed the way that people approached the arts. During the Renaissance, many wealthy people became patrons of the arts. They supported talented painters, sculptors, architects, and other artists.

Renaissance artists rediscovered the classical technique of perspective, which makes paintings look three-dimensional. Sculptors imitated the natural postures and expressions that they admired in Greek and Roman sculptures. Architects visited Roman ruins and created buildings in styles copied from Greece and Rome.

The Renaissance was also a wonderfully creative period for literature, particularly drama. The century from 1580 to 1680 was a golden age of theater in England, France, and Spain. It was during this time that the English writer William Shakespeare produced such plays as *Romeo and Juliet, A Midsummer Night's Dream,* and *Hamlet.*

A Revolution in Science

But it does move!

—Galileo, when forced to deny
the earth circles the sun

In the Middle Ages, scientific thought was based on the authority of ancient writings, such as the Bible or Greek and Roman writers. Following these ancient authorities, scholars believed that God had placed the earth at the center of the universe. The earth stood still, and the moon, sun, planets, and stars circled around it. By the mid-1500s, some thinkers began to question this view, and a scientific revolution took place.

Scientists began to go directly to nature. They observed how nature worked and thought out the truth for themselves. A Polish astronomer named Nicolaus Copernicus (koh•PUR•nuh•kuhs) studied the skies for 35 years. He concluded that the earth revolves around the sun. Afraid of the Church, he didn't publish his ideas until 1543, the year he died. In 1609, Galileo (gal•luh•LAY•oh) Galilei, an Italian astronomer, used a new Renaissance invention, the telescope, to study the heavens. What he saw supported Copernicus's ideas. Galileo was later forced by the Church to deny that the earth circles the sun. However, the scientific revolution could not be stopped.

Another Renaissance invention, the printing press, helped spread the ideas of the humanists. From its invention in about 1440 by a German craftsman named Johann Gutenberg, printing spread quickly to other cities in Europe. By 1500, presses in about 250 cities had printed between 9 and 10 million books. Printing helped spread the ideas and works of Renaissance thinkers, writers, and scientists throughout Europe.

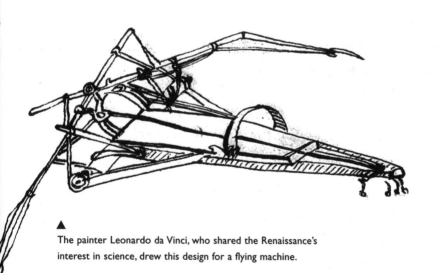

▲

The painter Leonardo da Vinci, who shared the Renaissance's interest in science, drew this design for a flying machine.

Reformation Europe, 1550

Power Struggles and Religious Wars

War is one of the scourges with which it has pleased God to afflict men.

—Cardinal Richelieu

During the Renaissance, Italy was a group of small, independent states. Some were controlled by a single city, such as Florence or Venice. The Papal states were ruled by the Pope, the head of the

Church in Rome. All these states fought constantly among themselves.

A scholar from Florence named Niccolò Machiavelli studied this violent world and wrote a book called *The Prince*. In it, he described what a ruler needed to do in order to succeed. He must, Machiavelli said, be as strong as a lion and as cunning as a fox.

In 1517 a German monk, Martin Luther, nailed a list of his criticisms of the Church to the door of a church in Wittenberg. His act started the Protestant Reformation. During much of the next 130 years, Europe was torn by religious conflict. Some regions remained solidly Catholic, such as Spain, Portugal, and the Italian states. Others became Protestant, such as England and Sweden. Some areas were strongly divided. In France, the conflicts between Catholics and the Protestant minority known as the Huguenots (HYOO•guh•NOTS) led to a long series of religious wars. The Holy Roman Empire was also divided between Protestant and Catholic. Again the result was war.

Brave New Worlds

I found very many islands peopled with inhabitants beyond number.

—Christopher Columbus

Trade and commerce brought riches to northern Italian cities like Florence and Venice. A new, wealthy class of merchants and bankers arose, with a taste for foreign luxury goods, such as silk and spices. Europeans sought new sea routes to replace ancient overland trade routes like the Silk Road. The Silk Road was a system of ancient caravan routes across Central Asia, along which traders carried silk and other goods. The Portuguese led the way into unknown worlds.

Under Prince Henry the Navigator, the Portuguese developed a new type of ship, the caravel (KAR•uh•VEHL). The caravel was a small, sturdy ship that could carry a lot of supplies and was easy to steer. It was well-suited for exploration. Throughout the 1400s, Portuguese sailors pushed farther and farther down the west coast of Africa. In 1498, Vasco da Gama sailed around Africa's tip to India and returned to Europe with a cargo of spices. The Portuguese later reached China and Japan.

▲

An artist of the 1800s pictures Magellan's ships near the tip of South America on their voyage around the world.

Other European nations imitated the Portuguese. In 1492, Christopher Columbus, an Italian sailing for Spain, crossed the Atlantic Ocean and reached the islands off the coast of the Americas. English and French voyagers explored North American coasts and rivers. In 1519–1522, a Spanish expedition led by Ferdinand Magellan was the first to sail around the world.

Time Line

1260–1294—In China, Kublai Khan encourages trade via the Silk Road.

1348—Bubonic plague strikes Florence.

1418–1434—Prince Henry sends Portuguese ships to Cape Bojador on the West African coast.

c. 1450—Johann Gutenberg invents the printing press.

1469–1492—Lorenzo de' Medici rules Florence and sponsors artists.

1483–1498—Torquemada leads the Spanish Inquisition.

1509–1547—Henry VIII rules England.

1519–1522—Magellan's crew sails around the world.

1556–1598—Philip II rules Spain.

1558–1603—Elizabeth I rules England.

1564–1616—William Shakespeare lives and writes in England.

1588—Sir Francis Drake defeats the Spanish Armada.

The World
of the Court

Federigo's Falcon

FROM BOCCACCIO'S *DECAMERON*

RETOLD BY WALTER HAZEN

Giovanni Boccaccio was the author of the **Decameron**
(1353), a very important literary work of the early Renaissance.
In this book, ten fashionable young people flee the plague
in Florence and go to the countryside. There they pass the
time by telling stories. For ten days, each of the group tells a
story.

"Your turn, Fiammetta," Filomena reminded
me. "It's your turn to tell a story."

And indeed it was. Eight people already had
told a story. Only Dioneo and I had not. I would be
the ninth and he the tenth.

People and Terms to Know

Giovanni Boccaccio (joh•VAHN•ee boh•KAH•chee•OH)—(1313–1375)
Italian writer.

Decameron (duh•KAM•uhr•uhn)—collection of 100 tales by Boccaccio.
The title, which means "ten days," refers to the time spent by
Boccaccio's fictional young people in storytelling.

A young noblewoman holds her falcon.

Five days ago, our group—seven young ladies and three young men—had fled from Florence, our home city. Now we are staying at a farm in the hills.

Why are we telling stories? In this year, 1348, a terrible **plague** has struck Florence. Every day, it kills thousands of people. We decided to escape to the countryside together. We hope that the plague won't reach us here. To calm ourselves and to pass the time, we take turns telling stories.

Here is my tale. It concerns a love-struck gentleman named Federigo. His love was a beautiful woman named Monna Giovanna (MOH•nuh joh•VAN•nuh), or "Lady Joanna." She was said to be one of the loveliest and most gracious women in Florence. She was married to a very wealthy man. Federigo believed in the traditions of **courtly love** and dedicated himself to Monna Giovanna in a pure way. He was quite rich, so he spent huge sums of money to gain her attention and favor. He put on

People and Terms to Know

plague (playg)—highly infectious, widespread disease. In the 1300s, the bubonic plague, called the Black Death, killed one-third of Europe's population and about 65 million people worldwide.

courtly love—idealized form of love popular in the courts of the Middle Ages and Renaissance. In courtly love, a knight or courtier devoted himself to a noble woman, who usually was married.

jousts and **tournaments**. He gave banquets and festivals. He sent her expensive gifts. But nothing he did impressed her. Alas! She paid no attention to him at all.

All of this spending soon made Federigo a poor man. His fortune was almost gone. All he had left was a prized **falcon** and a little farm in the country. Since he had failed to win Monna Giovanna's love, he moved to his farm. There he tried to live as modestly as possible.

After Federigo left Florence, Monna Giovanna's wealthy husband grew ill and died. Now she was a widow with a young son and a lot of money. Following the custom of the time, she left Florence and moved to her husband's estate in the country. This estate happened to be near Federigo's little farm.

It wasn't long before Monna Giovanna's son became friendly with Federigo. Soon the two were hunting together with Federigo's prized falcon. The boy loved the bird and wanted to own it. But he never mentioned it to Federigo, since Federigo loved the falcon so much.

People and Terms to Know

jousts—combats between two knights using lances.

tournaments—contests in which two groups of knights fight each other on horseback, using lances, swords, or other weapons.

falcon—bird with a short, curved beak and long, pointed wings. In the Middle Ages and Renaissance, falcons were trained to hunt game.

One day, Monna Giovanna's son fell ill. He became so sick that it looked like he would die. She sat by his bedside every day and comforted him. "What can I get for you?" she asked. "I promise to get you anything that you want, if it will help you to get well!"

"Federigo's falcon," the lad said one day. "I would like to have Federigo's falcon. If you can get it for me, Mother, I'm sure I will overcome this sickness."

> "I promise to get you anything that you want, if it will help you to get well!"

Monna Giovanna had no idea how she could get the falcon. How could she even think of going to Federigo? She had ignored his love. How could she ask him for the one possession that he still had? But she promised her son that she would. Her promise delighted the boy. He seemed better for having heard it.

So Monna Giovanna came up with a plan. She would go to visit Federigo at his little farm. But she would not go alone. She would take a lady friend. When they arrived, she would tell Federigo that she was sorry for the misery she had caused him. She would make up for it by having dinner with him.

When Monna Giovanna arrived, Federigo was beside himself with joy and happiness.

"Madam," he said, "your visit is more dear to me now than it would have ever been in the past. Here—you wait in the garden with the wife of my gardener. I will go tell my servant to prepare a dinner worthy of you."

Federigo hurried into the house to see that the meal was prepared. To his dismay, however, he discovered that there was nothing left to eat. He searched his whole house, looking for money to buy food for Monna Giovanna's dinner. But he found none. He thought about borrowing money from the gardener, but his pride stopped him from doing that. What was he to do? He was frantic. At long last, his lovely Monna Giovanna had come to him, and he could not afford to put even a simple meal on the table!

Then his eyes fell on his prized falcon sitting on its perch. Such a fat bird would be a fitting dinner for his beloved. Without a second thought, he grabbed the falcon and wrung its neck. Then he handed it to his servant girl. "Pluck and broil this for dinner," he said.

While the falcon cooked, Federigo busily prepared to welcome Monna Giovanna into his humble home. He had saved some of his finest linens. These he proudly placed on the table. Satisfied, he returned to the garden, where his guest and her friend were waiting.

"My modest dinner is ready," he happily reported, "if you will just follow me."

The three entered the house and sat down at the dining table. The two ladies, of course, had no idea that the plump bird they were eating was Federigo's falcon. They finished dinner and spoke pleasantly for a while. Then Monna Giovanna brought up the subject of the falcon.

"There is one thing that he has asked for. It is the one thing that could possibly save his life."

"Federigo," she began, "as you know, my son is quite ill. In fact, I am afraid he might die. But there is one thing that he has asked for. It is the one thing that could possibly save his life."

"And what is that?" Federigo asked.

"Your falcon," she replied. "He thinks that if he could have your falcon, it might give him the will to live."

At this, Federigo broke down weeping. He confessed that the fowl they had just eaten was the falcon of which she spoke. Hearing this, Monna Giovanna scolded him for wasting such a fine bird to please a woman. Then, her mood changed from anger to admiration. Here was a person who had sacrificed something he dearly loved for a lady he loved even more.

As was expected, Monna Giovanna's son soon died. She grieved for a long time. After that, she took her brothers' advice to remarry. Her brothers were surprised when she chose to marry Federigo. But they did not object. They knew him to be a good man.

At long last, Federigo was married to the woman he had loved for many years. He lived out his remaining days a happy man. He was also a rich man. Monna Giovanna brought her wealth to the marriage, too.

And that, dear friends, concludes my story.

QUESTIONS TO CONSIDER

1. In what ways did Federigo follow the traditions of courtly love?

2. Why did Monna Giovanna move to her husband's estate in the country?

3. If you had been Monna Giovanna, would you have felt responsible for Federigo wasting his fortune? Why or why not?

4. What do you learn about life in Italy at the time of this story?

The Renaissance: A First Book
by Neil Grant

Neil Grant introduces some of the most important people and events of the Renaissance.

The Renaissance
by James A. Corrick

James A. Corrick uses quotations from a wide variety of Renaissance documents to present the political, social, and cultural history of this period.

Old Neopolitan Fairy Tales:
Selected and Retold from *Il Pentamerone*
by Giambattista Basile (retold by Rose Laura Minicieli)

Like Boccaccio's Decameron, Giambattista Basile's Il Pentamerone is a great collection of Renaissance tales. Rose Laura Minicieli has selected and retold a number of Basile's tales.

Persecution in Spain

BY BARBARA LITTMAN

"Shh, Miguel. Someone might hear you! You know what happens to **heretics**? Do you want to end up like our cousin? Hauled off and tortured by the **Inquisition**!"

My brother Miguel has always been bolder than I am. He never was afraid of anyone. When we were kids, he fooled around in temple all the time. Our parents and the **rabbi** warned him to stop, but he never did. He didn't scare very easily. Lately, though,

---

People and Terms to Know

heretics (HEHR•ih•tihks)—people accused of heresy, that is, of believing things that went against the teachings of the Catholic Church.

Inquisition—from 1478 to 1808, formal investigation into people's beliefs by representatives of the Roman Catholic Church. Its goal was to find heretics and get rid of heresy. The Spanish government used the Inquisition to get rid of political enemies and as a way of control by terror.

rabbi (RAB•eye)—person trained in Jewish law, ritual, and traditions; Jewish religious leader.

An artist of the 1800s pictures heretics on their way to execution during

even Miguel has been afraid. These days, just about everyone is. You never know when someone might turn you in, even if you're innocent. That's what happened to our cousin, David. He was turned in.

Miguel, David, and I were born Jews. We had a hard life. We had to wear badges at all times, to show that we were Jewish. We were also forbidden to do many things. We couldn't even ride horses or shave! And at every turn, someone we knew was murdered just for being a Jew.

Now we're Christians, it's not much better. No one seems to trust us. We're called *conversos*, because we converted to Christianity. People watch us all the time to see if we've really given up our old religion. If they see anything suspicious, they report us. That's what happened to David. We're not sure what he was reported for, but he was hauled away. We haven't seen him for weeks.

Every time there is an **_auto da fé_** like this one, Miguel and I come. If we're not here, watching, someone might turn us in. Also, we hope to find out something about David.

People and Terms to Know

auto da fé (AW•toh duh FAY)—public meeting to announce the sentences of people found guilty by the Inquisition. In Portuguese, *auto da fé* means "act of faith." Often it was followed by executions, usually burning at the stake. The Church conducted the Inquisition, but the executions were done by government authorities.

Heretics being burned at an *auto da fé*.

We've been watching the heretics shuffle past. They're dressed in *sanbenitos*, the yellow sackcloths every heretic has to wear. You can tell whether a person has repented or not by what is painted on the *sanbenito*. Heretics who refuse to repent have frightening pictures of devils and the flames of hell painted on their sackcloths. They will die at the *auto da fé*.

Suddenly Miguel whispered loudly to me. "Look, look! There is David! Isn't that David? It can't be! Look at the pictures on his *sanbenito*!"

Until this very moment, I had hoped David would be let go. Now I know he will die. After what he's been through, maybe he is ready to die. One of my neighbors who was released told me about it.

First you're taken to the Casa Santa, the headquarters of the Inquisition. Inside, everything is black. There is no sunlight anywhere. You sit across a table from a panel of

If you won't admit to the crimes, you're tortured.

inquisitors. These men will lead the questioning about your beliefs. Their secretary reads out your crimes. If you won't admit to the crimes, you're tortured.

My neighbor was tortured. Her arms were tied behind her back and attached to a pulley. Then she was lifted off the floor. The inquisitors left her hanging for hours. They had many other kinds of torture, too. Many people who aren't heretics confess to crimes anyway just to stop the torture. My neighbor said the torture was horrible. People even turn in their friends and family to make it stop. That's why everyone is so scared.

My brother and I live in fear. We don't know who turned David in. Worse, we don't know why. If we do anything wrong, we could be next.

Tomás de Torquemada, the Grand Inquisitor, made a list of things that identify a person who is not a good Christian. For example, if you don't have smoke coming from your chimney on Saturday, that might mean that your family is observing the Jewish Sabbath, or holy day. On the Sabbath, we Jews do not light fires or cook.

Torquemada has power in Spain because Queen Isabella listens to him. He is her confessor, the priest that she confesses her sins to. Since he helped her become closer to God, she trusts him. Now, he wants her to use the Inquisition to rid Spain of anyone who isn't a good Catholic. This means all nonbelievers, Jews, and witches. It even means Muslims, although they have been in Spain for hundreds of years. Everywhere you look you see what they have done for Spain.

King Ferdinand thinks Torquemada is right. Some people say that the king and queen like the

People and Terms to Know

Tomás de Torquemada (TAWR•kuh•MAH•duh)—(1420–1498) monk who was Grand Inquisitor in Spain from 1483 to 1498. He used torture to identify heretics and made the Inquisition much harsher than it had been.

Isabella—Isabella I (1451–1504), ruler of the Spanish states of Castile and León (1474–1504). Her marriage to King Ferdinand II of Aragón helped to unify Spain.

Muslims—believers in Islam, a religion founded by the prophet Muhammad. Spain had many Muslims before they were forced out of the country in 1492.

Ferdinand—Ferdinand II (1452–1516), king of the Spanish state of Aragón (1479–1516). His marriage to Queen Isabella of Castile allowed them to join their lands and work successfully toward a united, strong Spain.

money they're getting from the Inquisition. They get all the property from convicted heretics. Many Jews in our community are bankers and business people, so they often are wealthy. It certainly pays to convict them of heresy! Money from the Inquisition is helping King Ferdinand fight his war against the Muslims in southern Spain.

"What will happen to Spain when all the Jews are gone?"

King Ferdinand is making a big mistake. Like the Muslims, the Jews have done a lot to help Spain. Jewish artists, philosophers, and writers have helped make Spain great. I ask myself all the time, "What will happen to Spain when all the Jews are gone?"

Torquemada is one of the inquisitors at today's *auto da fé*. He's sitting with the other inquisitors on the highest platform in the town square. There's a large green cross draped in black fabric. There's also an altar with lit candles and burning incense.

Some people say Torquemada is kind and is trying to help make Spain strong. When he was young, he was a pious monk who studied hard and made sacrifices to try to become holy. They explain that he thinks people will be more loyal if they have the same religion.

I don't care what they say. Terror grips my chest, as I watch him up there on the platform. He doesn't care how many people he tortures and kills. Today, my cousin David will die because of him. Next month, it may be me or Miguel.

Torquemada is looking down at the platform where the prisoners have been led. They each have two priests next to them—even David. His priests have been with him all night. They walked beside him as he was paraded into the town square. I know they've been trying to get him to confess. He's going to die by fire as punishment for his crimes. That can't be changed, but the Church wants to save his soul. Hah!

The prisoners' platform is draped in black cloth. Around the platform are straw dummies of some convicted heretics who escaped. Those will be burned, too.

Torquemada is just starting to perform **Mass** now. I've seen this before. When he's done with Mass, he'll preach a long sermon. This gives the accused more time to confess.

People and Terms to Know

Mass—central service of worship in the Roman Catholic Church.

When Torquemada is done with his sermon, his job will be done. It's true he has questioned and tortured people accused of heresy. He will not light the fire, though. Neither will any of the other priests or inquisitors. A representative of the law will lead the convicted to their fate.

Dusk is almost here. Everything will be done then. That is how the inquisitors plan it. They start each *auto da fé* at dawn and end it just before dusk. They don't want people milling about after dark.

My heart is very heavy. Soon this will be over, and David will be gone. I wish I could let David know we're here. I wish I could go home and never come to another *auto da fé*. But I am being watched. . . .

QUESTIONS TO CONSIDER

1. Who were the victims of the Inquisition?

2. Why did Ferdinand and Isabella support the Inquisition?

3. In what ways might the treatment of the Muslims and Jews have harmed Spain in the long run?

4. If you had lived in Spain during the Inquisition, how do you think you would have felt about what was happening?

The Spanish Inquisition

The Spanish Inquisition started in 1478.
It continued until 1834, when it was finally
outlawed. While Torquemada was Grand
Inquisitor, about 2,000 people were killed. In
1492, Torquemada convinced Ferdinand and
Isabella to sign an order that made more than
160,000 Jews leave Spain. They had to leave
their homes and most of their possessions
behind. Many of them were wealthy, educated
people who had helped to make Spain great.

Machiavelli's Advice to Rulers

BY JUDITH LLOYD YERO

Early in the 1500s, the brilliant, cruel <u>Cesare Borgia</u> was duke of Romagna (roh•MAHN•yuh), a region in northern Italy. Borgia ruled Romagna by terror. When the people rose up against him, he ordered a man named Remirro to bring them under control. Remirro crushed all resistance. Then Borgia decided that he didn't want to be blamed for what Remirro had done. One dark night, he had Remirro's body cut in half. He left it in the center of town.

What happened? The people of Romagna were glad to see Remirro punished. However, they were

---

People and Terms to Know

Cesare Borgia (CHAY•zahr•ay BAWR•juh)—(1476–1507) Italian ruler, soldier, and politician; son of the man who became Pope Alexander VI. The ruthless Cesare became a cardinal at 18 and may have had his own brother killed.

shocked by what Borgia had done. They would be careful not to cross him in the future. Both of these results were good for Cesare Borgia.

Was Borgia a wicked ruler? Most people felt he was a monster. But **Niccolò Machiavelli**, author of the famous work called **_The Prince_**, calls Borgia an example of the ideal ruler. As Machiavelli put it, "Politics have no relation to morals."

Machiavelli had other strong ideas about how leaders should act. Here are some of them:

> "If it's necessary to hurt people for the good of the state, do it all at once. The people will be angry at first, but will soon forget if their lives improve.

> "It's better to be feared than to be loved, but a leader shouldn't make the people hate him because that makes them dangerous.

> "A prudent ruler cannot, and must not, honor his word when it places him at a disadvantage.

People and Terms to Know

Niccolò Machiavelli (MAHK•ee•uh•VEHL•ee)—(1469–1527) Italian diplomat, political writer, and historian. Machiavelli is considered the founder of modern political science.

The Prince—famous and influential book by Machiavelli. It was written in 1513 and published in 1532.

Because men are wretched creatures who would not keep their word to you, you need not keep your word to them.

"A leader should always appear honest, generous and merciful, while doing whatever he has to do to keep his power.

"Be as cruel and ruthless as you have to in order to keep your power, but never admit that you've done anything wrong."

Where did Machiavelli get such ideas? To answer that, we must look at his life and the times in which he lived.

Niccolò Machiavelli was born in Florence, Italy, in 1469. Though his father came from a noble family, he was its poorest member. Machiavelli suffered from poverty growing up, but he managed to study law and the classics. He joined Florence's lawyers' **guild**.

Northern Italy included the **city-states** of Florence, Milan, and Genoa. Rival groups struggled

---

People and Terms to Know

guild (gihld)—association of people in the same trade. Guilds set standards for the quality of their work, described the training by which an apprentice could become a full member, and protected businesses from outside competition. See page 104.

city-states—independent, self-governing cities and the territory around them.

to gain control of these city-states. Spain, France, Germany, and the **papacy** also fought each other to control them.

While Machiavelli was growing up, Florence was a republic led by the Medicis, Italy's richest and most powerful family. **Lorenzo de' Medici** ruled Florence until 1492, bringing it to a high level of culture. But Lorenzo's son Piero, who followed him, was a weak ruler. The people of Florence drove the Medicis from the city in 1494 and appointed a Council of Ten to rule the city.

That year, Machiavelli entered public service. He was 25 years old. Within five years, he became an important official of the Florentine Council. Acting as a **diplomat**, Machiavelli visited many foreign courts. He met the famous and powerful rulers of France, Spain, and Germany. He also met the Italian warlord Cesare Borgia. Machiavelli watched how these rulers behaved. He formed ideas about what a successful ruler of a powerful country should and shouldn't do.

People and Terms to Know

papacy (PAY•puh•see)—Roman Catholic Church government headed by the pope.

Lorenzo de' Medici (MEHD•ih•chee)—(1449–1492) Italian ruler, poet, and patron of the arts, known as "Lorenzo the Magnificent." A member of a great Italian banking family, Lorenzo ruled Florence from 1469 to 1492. He supported such artists as Leonardo da Vinci and Michelangelo.

diplomat—person appointed to represent a government to other governments.

◀ Niccolò Machiavelli.

In 1512, at the height of Machiavelli's political career, the Medici family came back into power. Word got around that Machiavelli had plotted to overthrow the Medicis. He was arrested, thrown into prison, and tortured. He claimed to be innocent. At last, Machiavelli was released from prison, but he had to leave Florence.

Bitter and disappointed, Machiavelli moved to his farm outside of Florence. Now, suspected of treason, he was allowed only limited freedom to travel. His friends abandoned him, too, and he lost faith in human nature. As he later says in *The Prince*,

"It may be said of men in general, that they are ungrateful, fickle, deceivers, cowardly, greedy."

Machiavelli threw himself into a study of the great leaders of history. He spent hours each day in the "ancient courts of ancient men." Drawing on the lessons of history and his own experience in Europe's courts, Machiavelli started to write *The Prince*.

"How we live is far removed from how we ought to live."

Others had written high-sounding words about how great leaders *should* act. Machiavelli felt that strong leaders did not follow such rules. He said, "How we live is far removed from how we ought to live." In *The Prince*, Machiavelli describes how successful and powerful leaders of history *really* rule.

Whether Machiavelli approved of the actions of people like Cesare Borgia was unimportant. Machiavelli believed that the people suffered when a ruler was weak. Therefore, a leader should do anything that was necessary to keep a state strong.

Machiavelli dedicated his book to the Medici family. He closed *The Prince* by urging them to use his ideas to return Italy to its former glory.

In 1519 Machiavelli made peace with the Medicis and returned to Florence. There he continued to write works on history and politics. Machiavelli died in 1527, and *The Prince* was published after his death.

Did he really believe that rulers don't have to follow the moral laws that govern other people? Scholars still argue about what Machiavelli thought. What do you think?

QUESTIONS TO CONSIDER

1. What was Machiavelli trying to explain to rulers in *The Prince*?

2. What is your opinion of Machiavelli's idea that it is better for a ruler to be feared than loved?

3. In what kind of situation might people respect a leader who followed Machiavelli's advice?

4. How do you think a ruler should behave?

Proper Behavior

BY LYNNETTE BRENT

The sheriff opened my cell door and handed me a change of clothes. My torn suit had once been beautiful. I actually had passed as a noble! But my little game was long over. I took off the suit and put on my own clothing. Now I look like the simple tailor that I really am. Soon I will be a convict, known only as a thief and a liar.

How did I think I would ever get away with such a crazy idea? It was just that I was tired of being treated badly. The wealthy people that I serve every day treat me like a nobody. When I showed up at the contessa's party, none of them recognized me. Yet, I found out that it takes much more than fine clothes and clever conversation to pass as a noble.

I work as a tailor for the noble families in Venice. My sewing skills are known throughout the city. But my job doesn't pay well. Oh, how I'd love to live like the people who I sew for! They have their fine homes, servants, and lives of leisure. Why, I wondered, couldn't that be me? I am certainly well educated. My father spent all of his spare money making sure I got

Oh, how I'd love to live like the people who I sew for!

good schooling. I speak French as well as I speak my native Italian. My manners are fair enough. I certainly know not to offend my customers. And *I* would not take my riches for granted, as many of my clients do.

I had an appointment at the baron's castle to fit him for a new set of clothes. He wanted to look grand at the dinner party that a noblewoman, the contessa, was having. He wanted a fine suit to impress some visiting royalty. While I waited for him, I noticed a book on his table. Many of my customers had talked about it and the author, **Baldassare Castiglione**. Here it was, *The Book of*

People and Terms to Know

Baldassare Castiglione (BAHL•duh•SAHR•ee KAH•stihl•YOH•nay)— (1478–1529) Italian courtier and man of letters. Castiglione's *Book of the Courtier* was published in 1528.

the Courtier! I picked it up and started reading a few pages. It was full of conversations about how to be a **courtier**. It was as if an angel had placed the book in front of me! I slipped it into my bag and hurried to a chair at the other side of the room. I didn't want to raise suspicion if anyone noticed the book was missing.

I took the baron's order and then returned to my shop. Suddenly, I had a wonderful idea. If *The Book of the Courtier* told how a nobleman should behave, I could read it and pass myself off as a noble! And where better to test my plan than the contessa's party? What fun it would be to get away with this disguise! I could travel with new friends. I could dine with royalty. I could learn from artists. Why, I could even discuss military strategy with celebrated heroes.

Preparing for the party proved to be difficult. I needed to read Castiglione's book and know it by heart. I had less than three weeks. Each night I memorized a few pages. I had to be sure that I could join in any conversation without being found out.

People and Terms to Know

courtier (KAWR•tee•uhr)—noble person in attendance at a royal court.

Baldassare Castiglione.

There was a problem right away. The rules for being a courtier were very detailed and long. I couldn't possibly learn them all. Fortunately, there were large sections of the book on graceful behavior, sports, humor, and love. I would talk only about these topics. I'd find a way not to dance, sing, or play music. These were important to the courtier, but a monkey could make better music than I could!

"A courtier should play upon the lute, and sing to it with the lyrics."

The Book of the Courtier told in great detail how nobles should behave. It told about how they should speak around their prince. At first I thought that a nobleman should flatter and be overly kind to the prince. Instead, Castiglione recommended a nobleman be direct

_____

A nobleman is a servant to a prince, not an equal.

_____

and straightforward. It was also important not to look like you were asking for favors or gifts. A nobleman is a servant to a prince, not an equal.

"The courtier should not be a fond flatterer, nor be a babbler, brawler, or chatterer."

At this social event, I would need to know the current parlor games and how to be a good sport. I should also have a positive attitude. According to Castiglione, noblemen should be prepared to speak well on any subject.

"Be able to give good and believable reasons upon every matter."

But most of all, my whole manner would need to be graceful and natural.

"I would wish the courtier to have not only talent and beauty of face and figure, but also a certain grace that we call an 'air.'"

I studied night after night. I worried that I wouldn't remember so many rules! To help myself, I stitched words and phrases into the inside of my coat. I could simply pretend to straighten my jacket and peek inside to read them. Even so, I was getting quite nervous.

The night of the party, I arrived at the contessa's home. Her servant announced the fancy name I had given myself. I walked into the ballroom. A few people turned as I was announced, but no one seemed suspicious. I had passed the first test—I was a guest at the party! A servant offered me food and something to drink. I accepted. I had decided that I would eat the wonderful food right away. After all, I could get caught before the end of the evening!

I watched the people in the room. Everyone was very dignified. Some people were dancing, some were talking, and some were eating like me. The contessa was giving some guests a tour of her rose garden. I listened to as many conversations as I could. I wanted to be prepared to talk to anyone. Here it was—my chance to live my life as a nobleman!

Here it was—my chance to live my life as a nobleman!

Suddenly the gentleman sitting next to me spilled his drink. The stain spread all over my coat. He was so polite! He said he was sorry. He tried to clean up the mess—but without making a scene. I looked at him and—goodness! It was the baron himself! I tried to excuse myself, but he was firm.

"Take off your coat, sir! Please let me see that this gets cleaned!" He clearly was upset. I feared looking the baron in the eye—he might recognize me! He tugged at my coat, trying to be helpful. Terror seized me. I tried to stop him. He might see the words sewn into the lining!

Suddenly, we heard a "Rrrrrip." The sleeve had torn off. The baron looked horrified. For all he knew, he had ripped the coat of a distinguished gentleman. For a minute, I thought I would be safe.

"Direct all things to a good end."

"Oh, dear!" cried the baron. "I will see to it that this is repaired, good as new. I know a wonderful tailor."

I couldn't believe it—he was talking about me! (At least he had kind words for me.)

The baron turned toward me, his face red with embarrassment. But what happened next made my heart sink. The look on the baron's face suddenly changed from concern to anger. He recognized me! I had gotten a good meal—but I was no longer a welcome guest.

QUESTIONS TO CONSIDER

1. What was the purpose of Castiglione's *Book of the Courtier*? Why do you think that he wrote such a book?

2. What were some of the topics in his book?

3. If Castiglione were alive today, what topics would you expect him to include in a book about how to behave as a government official or staff member?

4. What do you learn from this story about life in Venice in the 1500s?

The Six Wives of Henry VIII

BY MARIANNE McCOMB

Please deliver this letter in all haste to His Royal Highness, King **Henry VIII**, Hampton Court, Surrey.

January 1543

Your Royal Highness,

You have very kindly asked for my advice on whether you should marry **Catherine Parr**. Let me begin by thanking you a thousand times for the opportunity. You have always been very kind to me, sire. I see that you are continuing your fine

---

People and Terms to Know

Henry VIII—(1491–1547) king of England (1509–1547).
Catherine Parr—(1512–1548) sixth and last wife of Henry VIII of England. Theirs was a loving relationship that lasted four years until his death. Before proposing, the king asked advisors what they thought. Most people said he should marry Catherine.

In a drawing from the 1800s, Henry VIII is surrounded by his six wives,
(clockwise from the top) Anne of Cleves, Catherine Howard, Anne Boleyn,
Catherine of Aragón, Catherine Parr and Jane Seymour.

record. You are truly the greatest ruler in all England's history. But of course you know that, sire. You've said it often enough yourself.

First of all, I hope that my opinion of Catherine Parr matches yours. I've made it a point to always agree with you in the past. I see no reason to change this habit now.

> *A marriage, you say, must be made with one eye on politics and the other eye on the cradle.*

Your Highness, because you are so brilliant, you already know that marriage has very little to do with romance. Many times I've heard you share your wise opinion on the subject. A marriage, you say, must be made with one eye on politics and the other eye on the cradle. I so agree.

For this reason, sire, I believe that Catherine Parr could be the perfect sixth wife for you. Her family is quite powerful in England. This will help you in your efforts to strengthen your kingdom. Also, the lady is still of child-bearing age. Imagine how pleased you would be to have a younger brother for His Royal Highness, Prince **Edward**.

Sire, I agree with you that your first five wives were not what you expected or deserved. Of course, this was through no fault of yours. Those miserable women! How could they not have seen your brilliance and generosity? They were blind, sire, blind!

Shall I review for you the problems with your past five marriages? You remember these problems all too well, of course. But allow me to save you the bother of thinking about them.

Your first wife, Catherine of Aragón, seemed like a good choice at the time. She was the daughter of Ferdinand and Isabella, the rulers of Spain. Because of your marriage with Catherine, England gained a wonderful **alliance** with Spain. Sire, think of how valuable that alliance has been for your kingdom!

People and Terms to Know

Edward—(1537–1553) Edward VI, son of Henry VIII's third wife, Jane Seymour. He became king in 1547. He was young and sickly, and let powerful nobles influence his rule. After his death at 16, his half-sister Mary became queen of England.

alliance (uh•LY•uhns)—formal agreement or treaty between two or more nations to cooperate for specific purposes.

But, alas, Catherine of Aragón could not give you a male heir. Although she gave birth to six children, only one survived. The surviving child, Princess **Mary**, was not the boy you had hoped for. And the Lady Anne Boleyn was pregnant with your child. So your decision to divorce Catherine was very wise. It's a shame that the pope would not permit a divorce. But you solved that problem by breaking from the Catholic Church altogether. This was a most excellent move, sire. You set up our Church of England. You are truly a gifted leader!

Your second wife, Anne Boleyn, was one of the great beauties of the kingdom. Still, there were many in your court who did not like her. Alas, she too was unable to give birth to a baby boy. You were kind enough to stay married to her for three long years. No one could say you weren't patient!

Many said Queen Anne was unfaithful to you. An assembly of 26 **peers** agreed unanimously!

People and Terms to Know

Mary—(1516–1558) Mary I. Mary became queen of England in 1553. She was known as "Bloody Mary" because she had hundreds of Protestants executed in an attempt to restore the Catholic Church in England.

peers—English noblemen known as "peers of the realm." They hold government office in England's Parliament, in the House of Lords.

The courts sentenced her to die, and her enemies in the court were thrilled. I'll never forget their look of satisfaction on the day that she was beheaded. Well done, Your Highness!

One day later, you were engaged to the capable Jane Seymour. Sire, I compliment you for moving so quickly! Queen Jane was an excellent choice as a third wife. She gave you an heir almost immediately. His Royal Highness, Prince Edward, was the happy result of this marriage. Queen Jane's death twelve days after the birth of the prince was heartbreaking for you and for the entire kingdom.

After Queen Jane died, you had the excellent idea of watching a "beauty parade" before choosing your next wife. Unfortunately, the beauties of the world would not go along with this idea. So your advisors convinced you to marry Anne of Cleves in the hopes that the marriage would lead to an alliance with Germany.

Sire, I remember how disappointed you were with Queen Anne. Who could blame you? She was dull and plain and she refused to learn English. I wasn't surprised for a moment when you decided that you would not share the royal bed. Just as you predicted, your marriage to Anne of Cleves was "a great yoke to enter into," and I don't blame you for being furious with your advisors. As punishment, you had one of them beheaded and asked the Church of England to **annul** the marriage. Thank heavens, that marriage only lasted six months!

On the day that your advisor was executed, you married the lovely Catherine Howard. I do believe that you loved her for a short time. That foolish girl and her family—what trouble they've caused. Her uncle, Thomas Howard, the Duke of Norfolk, was also Anne Boleyn's uncle. First he supports your marriage to his niece Anne. Then when everyone could see what *she* was, he presides at her trial. (He wanted to come out on the right side of *that* every which way.) And then, for mercy's sake, he puts forth another niece—Catherine. And she's the same sort! Well, when she was accused, she couldn't help but confess. The evidence was overwhelming! So, of course, off with her head! Who could blame you? And of

The evidence was overwhelming! So, of course, off with her head!

People and Terms to Know

annul (uh•NUL)—cancel formally.

---

course, that took care of Thomas Howard as well. How could you possibly have him around you after that!

This brings me to the present day. I encourage you to take a sixth wife. You've been single now for eighteen months—a lifetime to you, I am sure!

I hope that you will listen to the recommendations of your advisors and marry the intelligent and very capable Catherine Parr. I believe that she could be a companion to you for the rest of your life. More important, she shows no sign of being a fool, as many of your previous wives were. Catherine Parr would make a fine stepmother to your children, sire. She would give His Royal Highness, Prince Edward, all the respect and affection he deserves.

Thank you again for the chance to advise you. I remain—

Your ever-humble, ever-grateful, and ever-faithful servant,

Sir William Gardiner

Spiritual Advisor to His Royal Highness

King Henry VIII

QUESTIONS TO CONSIDER

1. How can you tell that Sir William Gardiner is a fictional character?

2. How would you describe Gardiner's advice?

3. What did you learn from this letter about royal marriages in Henry VIII's time?

4. Which of Henry VIII's marriages would you consider a "success"? Which would you consider "failures"? Use evidence from the letter to support your opinions.

King Henry VIII
by Robert Green

Robert Green's brief biography provides an introduction to the life and reign of Henry VIII.

Tudor Odours
by Mary J. Dobson

From London's slum streets to the country homes of the wealthy, England was a rather smelly place in the 1500s. Mary J. Dobson presents social history from an unusual angle, describing the way England smelled in Henry VIII's time.

The Prince and the Pauper
by Mark Twain

Mark Twain's classic tale tells how King Henry VIII's son Prince Edward and the beggar Tom Canty discover that they look exactly alike. The two boys decide to swap identities for a momentary adventure. Then an accident forces each to survive the other's way of life.

The Family of Henry VIII

Henry VIII (1491–1547) became king 1509.

Catherine of Aragón (1485–1536) married 1509; bore daughter Mary 1516; divorced 1533.

Anne Boleyn (c. 1507–1536) married 1533; bore daughter Elizabeth 1533; executed 1536.

Jane Seymour (c. 1509–1537) married 1536; bore son Edward 1537; died following childbirth 1537.

Anne of Cleves (1515–1557) married 1540; marriage annulled 1540.

Catherine Howard (c. 1521–1542) married 1540; executed 1542.

Catherine Parr (1512–1548) married 1543. remarried 1547; died in childbirth 1548.

Mary I (1516–1558) daughter of Henry VIII and Catherine of Aragón; became queen 1553; married Philip II of Spain 1554; died childless 1558.

Elizabeth I (1533–1603) daughter of Henry VIII and Anne Boleyn; became queen 1558; died childless 1603.

Edward VI (1537–1553) son of Henry VIII and Jane Seymour; became king 1547; died childless 1553.

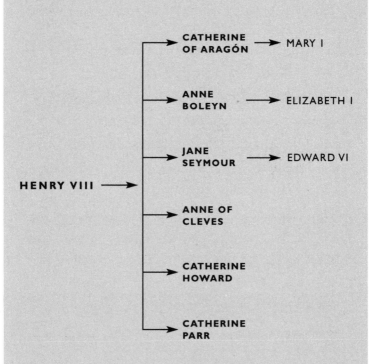

Elizabeth I and Her Age

BY STEPHEN FEINSTEIN

It happened years ago, when I was six. Mother woke me early one Saturday morning.

"Robert," said Mother. "Hurry and get dressed! Today, we're going to see our new queen!"

Father joined her in the doorway. He explained that at the **coronation** tomorrow, Princess **Elizabeth** would become queen. Today, the people could watch Elizabeth's coronation procession pass through London's streets. My father explained that this would be a wonderful parade.

People and Terms to Know

coronation—ceremony in which a ruler is crowned.

Elizabeth—Elizabeth I (1533–1603) queen of England who ruled from 1558 to 1603. Elizabeth was the daughter of King Henry VIII and Anne Boleyn. Her reign was one of England's greatest periods.

This portrait of Elizabeth was painted at the time of her coronation.

After breakfast, my parents bundled me up, and out we went. We must have walked at least a mile. Finally, we found a spot on the procession route. It was only mid-morning, but crowds of people already lined both sides of the street.

Hours went by, and I grew tired and bored. Suddenly, the sounds of the crowd grew much louder. A man next to us shouted, "Here she comes!" People on all sides were shouting and cheering in excitement.

Father lifted me up onto his shoulders. What a sight! Leading the procession was the queen herself, wearing a golden robe. She rode in an open carriage, pulled by horses decorated in gold draperies. Men carrying great battle-axes marched at her side. So did a great many servants dressed in crimson and silver. Behind the queen, a huge, thundering army of men on horseback stretched back as far as I could see.

I could not take my eyes off Elizabeth. She was only twenty-five years old then. I had never seen such beauty—her face, her amazing red-gold hair, the crown of a princess. Elizabeth smiled and waved to the people right and left.

As she passed in front of us, she stopped. She looked straight at me and asked me my name. I opened my mouth, but no sounds came out.

My father came to my rescue. "The lad's name is Robert, Your Grace," he said. The queen smiled at me, wished us well, and moved on. I sat staring after her, my heart pounding. That was the first time I met Queen Elizabeth, but it would not be the last.

As a young man, I joined a group of actors that traveled from town to town putting on plays. At first I helped the actors with their costumes. Before long, I became an actor.

Our group performed all over England at country fairs and at the great estates of the nobles. One day, we arrived at the country estate of Lord Clifford. We learned that we would perform for the queen that night.

During the afternoon, there was a break in our practice for the play. I took a walk with Rupert, a fellow actor. It was peaceful and quiet, except for the chirping of robins. We walked a long way, leaving the beautiful stone house behind us. While we admired the scenery, a procession came down the road toward us.

"Look! It's the queen!" said Rupert. Sure enough, it was Elizabeth and her entire court. The queen was riding on a horse, as were her courtiers and advisors. Behind them came hundreds of carts filled with luggage, supplies, and even furniture. "She must be on progress," Rupert added.

"Progress? What does that mean?" I asked. "Has she abandoned London? Is there something wrong?"

> *"Few of England's rulers have cared so much about our people."*

Rupert laughed. "No. Every summer, the queen goes on progress. She travels to different parts of England, visiting estates and villages along the way. She gets a welcome change of scenery and she gets to know her **subjects**, poor and rich alike. Few of England's rulers have cared so much about our people."

"We actors probably wouldn't have work without her, either," I said.

"Yes, that's true!" said Rupert. "Elizabeth certainly has helped the theater to grow. She has supported painters, poets, and musicians, too! Nobles certainly wouldn't be inviting us to their estates to give plays if the queen didn't like them so much!"

People and Terms to Know

subjects—people who are under the rule of a government leader, such as a king or a queen.

Suddenly, the queen stopped and beckoned to me. Once again, I gazed at her flaming red-gold hair and beautiful face. She asked how much farther it was to Lord Clifford's house. I opened my mouth to answer. But, just as when I was six, no words came forth. Elizabeth frowned, growing impatient. She asked me my name.

Rupert said, "His name is Robert, Your Grace. Lord Clifford's house is just yonder, around the bend." The queen galloped off, and the procession followed.

I stood there blushing and feeling like a complete fool. "Don't worry," said Rupert. "You're not the first actor to get stage fright! Just don't forget your lines tonight!" We headed back to the house to finish our rehearsal.

That evening, our play was a total success. I played my part superbly. The noble audience, dressed in fine clothes and glittering jewelry, clapped and cheered often. The queen laughed at the funny parts and clapped loudly at the end. She came up to congratulate us on our performance.

She smiled at me and, raising one brow, greeted me by name. My heart raced, and my face flushed.

Musicians began to play, and the royal guests happily began dancing. I marveled at the queen's energy. She danced on into the night. Rupert said that the queen's love of dancing was equaled only by her love of riding and hawking. No doubt, that is how she would spend the next day. The evening's grand climax came when Lord Clifford delighted everyone with a spectacular fireworks display.

During the next few years, plays became wildly popular in England, though some people, like the **Puritans**, opposed the theater. Elizabeth set up her own theater company, in part to silence these critics.

Elizabeth is well educated and knows several languages. Under her rule, the arts, science, business, trade, and industry all have grown. The queen has helped the poor and unemployed. She has made the English crown more powerful. She's kept us out of unnecessary wars and brought religious peace to England. She is an inspiring leader.

People and Terms to Know

Puritans—members of a group in the Church of England during the 1500s and 1600s who wanted simpler worship and stricter morals.

▲
Queen Elizabeth enjoying hunting game birds with trained hawks. Hawking was a popular sport in her time.

The last time I saw Queen Elizabeth was in July 1588. My group of actors was performing in Tilbury, on the southeast coast of England. At the time, Elizabeth was facing her greatest trial as ruler of England. **Philip II**, king of Spain, had sent

People and Terms to Know

Philip II—(1527–1598) king of Spain who reigned from 1556 to 1598. He was the strongest ruler in Europe at the time. Under him, the Spanish Inquisition reached its height. Although married to Elizabeth's sister Mary, he had never been crowned king of England. After Mary's death he tried to marry Elizabeth, but she wanted to keep power and would not marry.

his mighty **Spanish Armada** to attack England. The English fleet had sailed out to meet the Spaniards. The English army camped along the shore near Tilbury, ready to defend the coast.

I went to the camp to see what was going on. I wanted to see the Armada. Suddenly a mighty cheer went up from the assembled soldiers dressed in their armor. I turned to see who they were cheering. I gasped. It was our queen, riding a white horse!

"I have the heart and stomach of a king, and a king of England, too!"

She was dressed as a warrior. She wore a silver breastplate over a white velvet dress. She was bareheaded, and a page was carrying her helmet.

"I know I have the body of a weak and feeble woman," she cried, "but I have the heart and stomach of a king, and a king of England, too!" She dared any other nation to attack England. She would take up arms herself, if need be.

People and Terms to Know

Spanish Armada (ahr•MAH•duh)—King Philip II's fleet of warships. The Spanish Armada consisted of 130 ships, 8,000 sailors, and 19,000 soldiers. The English defeated them in 1588.

I joined the soldiers in crying, "God bless the queen!" Then Elizabeth noticed me standing near her. She told me I looked familiar and asked me my name. Without hesitation this time, I shouted gratefully, "My name is Robert, Your Grace! Long live the queen!"

QUESTIONS TO CONSIDER

1. What kind of person was Queen Elizabeth I?
2. What do you think that Elizabeth gained from going on her annual summer progress?
3. What did Queen Elizabeth accomplish during her reign?
4. How would Elizabeth's style as a governing leader work in the United States today?

Elizabethan England
by Ruth Ashby

Ruth Ashby introduces the history, culture, religion, and social conditions of England during the reign of Queen Elizabeth I.

Elizabeth I, Red Rose of the House of Tudor
by Kathryn Lasky

Kathryn Lasky's historical novel is told in the form of a series of entries from a diary kept by the future queen of England when she is an 11-year-old princess.

Behind the Mask: The Life of Queen Elizabeth I
by Jane Resh Thomas

Jane Resh Thomas's account of the life and times of Queen Elizabeth I presents the human being as well as the ruler.

Renaissance Art and Literature

Words into Print

BY STEPHEN CURRIE

St. Scholastica Monastery, Germany, 1355

Such a brilliant fall day, thought Brother Bernhard as he hurried along the path. Above his head, leaves stood out red and gold against the bright blue sky. In the nearby fields, farmers sang as they harvested their crops. Someone was baking bread in the **monastery** kitchens. The pleasant smell mixed with the scent of the herbs growing in the monastery garden. It was good to be alive on such a wonderful day as this, Brother Bernhard thought.

People and Terms to Know

monastery (MAHN•uh•STEHR•ee)—home for monks, men who take vows to devote their lives to religion and to live, work, and pray together. Before the invention of the printing press, some monasteries specialized in copying books by hand.

In an early printing shop, some workers (front) operate presses, while others (rear) set type.

First, though, came work. Brother Bernhard opened the door to the monastery workroom. The smell of herbs and bread was gone, replaced by the smells of **parchment**, ink, and pens. Brother Bernhard breathed deeply. Ahhh. Fifty-eight years old last March, he thought with a smile, and more than forty of them spent in the monastery. He still loved what he did.

Silently he slipped into his usual spot between Brother Gottlieb and Brother Kurt. The brothers nodded to him, but no one spoke. They were all hard at work, and conversation led to careless mistakes. Years ago, some young **novice** had been copying "Thou shalt not steal" from the Ten Commandments and had left out the word "not." Who did that? Brother Bernhard could not remember. But that young man had not lasted long.

People and Terms to Know

parchment—paper-like material made from animal skins that was often used in the preparation of books during the Middle Ages and the Renaissance.

novice (NAHV•ihs)—person who has entered a religious order but has not yet taken final vows.

St. Scholastica, high above the Rhine River near the city of Mainz, was well known in all of Germany for its book-copying. True, there were other monasteries and even a few copyists who were not monks. They all did reasonable work. But their work was not like St. Scholastica's. These monks were careful craftsmen with the most beautiful **calligraphy** anywhere. Few people could afford a book, Brother Bernhard knew. But many of those who could, chose St. Scholastica.

In over forty years, he had copied several Bibles and more prayer books. Each was a work of art.

They were never disappointed. The monastery's future was bright, Brother Bernhard told himself, and it was partly due to his skill. In over forty years, he had copied several Bibles and more prayer books. Each was a work of art.

He opened the Bible he was working on and dipped his pen into the ink. He made the first careful stroke onto the thick parchment. With hard work, care, and patience, he might manage to finish another page today.

People and Terms to Know

calligraphy (kul•LIHG•ruh•fee)—beautiful handwriting, often involving curls and other small lines, which was frequently used in manuscripts copied by monks.

St. Scholastica Monastery, 1455

"Total nonsense, if you ask me," Brother Werner sniffed.

"And yet—" began Brother Franz, a frown crossing his face.

"A fad," interrupted Werner. "It will never last." He quickened his step and hurried past the herb garden, while Franz struggled to keep up.

Their supper of bread and cheese was over. The dishes had been cleared away. The books sat patiently in the workroom, awaiting the next day of copying. Tomorrow, right after the monks' morning prayers, Werner would begin work on the title page of his **psalm book**. He planned to use real gold leaf and plenty of beautiful red dyes. His palms itched. Werner couldn't wait for sunrise to come.

But that was tomorrow. Today was different. This was the hour for exercise, just before evening prayers, and somehow he had wound up walking with Franz. Franz was a young monk, full of crazy ideas that made Werner's head ache.

People and Terms to Know

psalm (sahlm) **book**—book containing the Psalms, a group of 150 sacred songs and poems that make up a book of the Bible.

Werner gazed at the trees in the gathering twilight, the gold leaves and the red, and wished for the morning. "A printing press!" he said with disgust. "It will never work."

Franz blinked. "Oh, but I think it will," he said shyly. "Herr **Gutenberg** has invented a revolutionary new method of—"

Gutenberg, Gutenberg. Werner sighed. That was all Franz could talk about—a man named Johann Gutenberg, who had grown up just down the river in Mainz. According to Franz, Gutenberg had been a goldsmith who liked machinery. With a partner, Gutenberg had gone off to Strasbourg, some distance away. There Gutenberg had worked secretly for weeks, months, maybe even years, to build a machine that could print papers, bulletins, and books. (Franz always got very excited at this point in the story, and his eyes blinked even more rapidly than usual.)

Anyhow, Gutenberg was now back in Mainz, hard at work showing off his machine. Werner had seen a crude drawing of the press. It had made no sense to him at all. In his eyes, the machine just

---

People and Terms to Know

Gutenberg (GOOT•uhn•BURG)—(c. 1390–1468) Johann Gutenberg, German craftsman and inventor who invented a way of printing with movable type. Gutenberg's printing press was one of the most important inventions in world history. *Herr* is German for "mister."

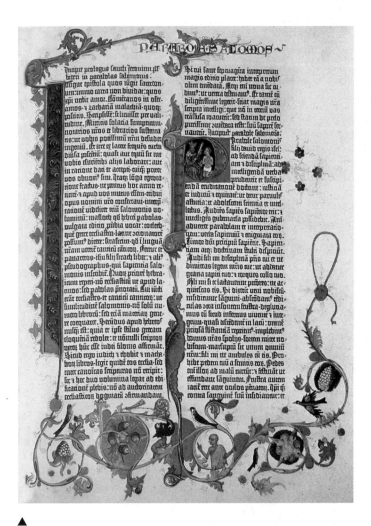

A page from a Gutenberg Bible shows its elaborate borders and decorated capital letters, which were added later by hand.

looked bulky, clunky, and inky, and what was the point of that? As far as Werner could tell, Gutenberg carved letters into brass and filled them with molten lead. Then he painted everything with gallons of ink and shoved great quantities of paper into the machine. A handle brought the wooden arm of the machine down to press the letters on the paper. Something like that, anyway. Werner wrinkled his nose. It sounded messy, dangerous, too.

"It will change the way we think about books," Franz was saying. "You can use the same metal letters again and again. Take the letters you need and put them in the right order. Then spread them with ink and press them against clean paper. Why, you can do dozens of pages in an hour! Move the letters to spell out the next page and—"

Werner sighed again. In his mind he could hear the letters clanking against one another. That's a much harsher sound than the comforting sound of the pen gliding across the parchment. "So your precious Herr Gutenberg can make dozens of pages in an hour," he interrupted. "Will these pages have gold leaf and beautiful red dyes?"

"No," Franz said, blinking again. "The first letters of chapters might have two colors. Printing in more than that would be complicated. But pages can have borders. And Herr Gutenberg says that someday—"

"Will there be calligraphy?" Werner interrupted.

"Yes, of course," Franz said, and he blinked several times, very fast. "The letters should look fine and fancy, says Herr Guten—"

"But they won't have the personal touch," Werner said triumphantly, drowning out the sound of Herr Gutenberg's name. "Do you know, I can look at a book and tell who copied it? The pen strokes, you know. The style of calligraphy. The spacing of the letters. Can your Herr Gutenberg match that?"

"No," Franz admitted. "But the point is to produce the books quickly and—"

"Will each of the books be different? Unique?" snapped Werner.

Franz blinked and shook his head. "No, they'll all be exactly the same. You see, the idea is—"

Werner stretched out his arms. "So your Herr Gutenberg is making people books that look just like everybody else's. Who would want such a book? They can come here and have their own beautiful copies made for them!"

The workroom was in sight, and the sun was beginning to set over the broad river. Franz clasped his hands behind his back. "I agree that our books are beautiful. They are personal, too.

But not everyone can afford a book from St. Scholastica. And we cannot copy quickly enough to give a book to everyone who wants one."

Franz blinked and gazed off across the Rhine. "We are in a time of great change, you know. All over Europe, creative people are making new art, poetry, music, and drama. New ideas are floating in the air! Don't you feel it? Things have stayed the same for centuries, but times are changing. We must change along with them. St. Scholastica has a history of making beautiful books, but Herr Gutenberg says—" And he was off again.

"New ideas are floating in the air! Don't you feel it?"

Werner gave up listening. Books weren't for everyone. They were only for priests and monks, scholars and the wealthy. The common people couldn't even read, so why did they need books? Werner's heart swelled with pride as he thought of the psalm book he had been copying for the last year. A wonderful piece of work, he told himself. That book truly was a work of art.

Franz could keep Herr Gutenberg and his silly ideas. If there was one certainty in this world, Werner thought, it was St. Scholastica.

Generations from now, when Herr Gutenberg and his banging, clanging printing press had been forgotten, the monks at St. Scholastica would be copying books.

That was certain!

St. Scholastica Monastery, 1555

"And what made you decide to join St. Scholastica?" asked Brother Andreas.

"The work you do, sir," answered the young man sitting opposite him. "I've seen your workroom and—"

Brother Andreas smiled. "Yes, we certainly are expert when it comes to herbs." He handed the man a printed list of the herbs grown at St. Scholastica, along with their uses. "Take this for fever, take that for toothache. . . . We like to say that our work here is to heal both in body and in spirit. We grow herbs to help the flesh and pray to help the soul."

"You do it well," said the young man, looking at the dozens of books on herbs lined up on the nearby shelf. "You must have been working with herbs here for years and years."

"Not exactly," Brother Andreas admitted. "Why, only a hundred years ago we specialized in the copying of books. That was back before Gutenberg and the printing press. It was back before printers could turn out one book after another, as one leaf after another turns orange and gold in the autumn. It was back before books were available to everyone, no matter how poor."

The young man's mouth flew open. "You mean there was a time when people copied books by hand?"

"There was," said Brother Andreas. "Bizarre, isn't it?"

QUESTIONS TO CONSIDER

1. Why did Brother Franz think that the printing press was important and valuable?

2. Why did Brother Werner oppose making books with a printing press?

3. How do you think that the invention of the printing press changed the way people read and thought about books?

4. If you had lived around 1500, how do you think you would have felt about printed books?

5. What modern inventions can you think of that some people think are only a fad and others think are here to stay?

Gutenberg
by Leonard Everett Fisher

Leonard Everett Fisher presents an introduction to the career of the man responsible for one of the most important inventions in history.

Breaking into Print: Before and After the Invention of the Printing Press
by Stephen Krensky

Stephen Krensky describes both what books were like before Gutenberg's invention and the effect of the printing press on civilization.

Bibles and Bestiaries: A Guide to Illuminated Manuscripts for Young Readers
by Elizabeth B. Wilson

Before Gutenberg invented the printing press, books were copied by hand. Elizabeth B. Wilson describes how a book was crafted in the Middle Ages.

Renaissance Man

BY DEE MASTERS

Caterina was young, beautiful, and poor when she gave birth to her son Leonardo on April 15, 1452. The baby's father, Ser Piero, was a young man from a wealthy family. Caterina and Ser Piero never married each other.

This child, **Leonardo da Vinci**, grew up to be one of the greatest artists, scientists, and inventors that the world has ever seen. Later generations would call him a **Renaissance man** because of his enormous talent and because he was interested in everything and wanted to do everything.

People and Terms to Know

Leonardo da Vinci (VIN•chee)—(1452–1519) outstanding artist, scientist, and inventor from the Italian city of Florence.

Renaissance man—one who has broad intellectual interests and is well versed in both the arts and the sciences.

The Renaissance was the age of exploration and Leonardo da Vinci was an explorer. He showed Europe that the world of possibilities was almost limitless.

Leonardo lived with his mother as an infant. But when he was about two, he moved to his father's country house, where his grandparents and his sixteen-year-old uncle, Francisco, raised him. Leonardo went into the olive groves, the grape vineyards, and the wheat fields with his uncle as Francisco ran the family estate. Leonardo observed and drew pictures of what he saw. The country priest taught him reading, writing, and arithmetic.

The Renaissance was the age of exploration and Leonardo da Vinci was an explorer.

When Leonardo was fourteen, his grandparents died, and his uncle Francisco married. As a result, Leonardo's father brought him to Florence to be an **apprentice**. Leonardo didn't have much of an education. Because his parents had never married, the laws would not allow him to go to college or to work at many jobs. What work could he do?

People and Terms to Know

apprentice—person who works under a skilled craftsman to learn a trade. See page 104 for more about apprentices.

As soon as Ser Piero saw the drawings of birds and plants that his son had made, he took them to the greatest artist in Florence, **Andrea del Verrocchio**. Leonardo became one of his apprentices.

Verrocchio's workshop was exciting. Verrocchio and his artists painted and sculpted. They also made bells, altars, decorations for homes, armor, swords, jewelry, and other things. The workshop was open to the street, and the streets of Florence were filled with the life and excitement of the Renaissance. Wealthy citizens and foreign traders passed through the city's streets. They brought goods from Asia, Africa, the Middle East, and from all over Europe. Powerful men and women in silk and velvet clothing ordered work from Verrocchio's studio.

Verrocchio directed everything. Men poured melted metal for cannons. Older apprentices used hammers and chisels to turn a block of stone into the statue of a famous man. One worker stood before an easel, painting a portrait of a wealthy man's family. Verrocchio checked plans for the construction of a

---

People and Terms to Know

Andrea del Verrocchio (vuh•ROH•kee•oh)—(1435–1488) sculptor and painter. His most important works are church decorations, statues, and figure and portrait sculpture.

---

bell tower and the bell to go in it. In one corner, a girl flirted with some of the older apprentices. A man with a tray came in, selling candy.

Leonardo and the other apprentices lived above the workshop and worked long, hard days. At first, Leonardo cleaned paintbrushes and swept the floor. He learned to grind up a blue stone to make blue paint, a yellow flower for yellow. For one shade of brown, he had to grind up pieces from Egyptian mummies! The apprentices compared their drawings. They argued over design ideas and shared new skills. Artists from all over came to talk, work, and learn at the workshop.

As he got older and more skillful, Leonardo started painting backgrounds for Verrocchio's pictures. In 1472, at the age of twenty, he became a Master Craftsman. One story says he painted an angel in one of Verrocchio's paintings. According to the story, when Verrocchio saw that the angel was the best part of the picture, he never painted again!

Ten years later, in 1482, Leonardo asked the powerful duke of Milan, **Ludovico Sforza**, for a job.

People and Terms to Know

Ludovico Sforza (SFAWRT•suh)—(1452–1508) powerful Italian prince. Sforza's court at Milan was one of the most splendid in Europe.

Many great Renaissance princes such as Sforza hired musicians, artists, and actors to entertain them, to decorate their homes and public buildings, and to show off their wealth.

To impress the duke, Leonardo made a silver **lute** shaped like a horse's head, and then he played it and sang. But he wasn't selling his artistic talents. Leonardo presented a letter to Sforza, applying for the job of military engineer. He said he could destroy any kind of fortress, make tunnels under walls without being heard, and cover wagons so they could not be attacked. He could invent machines. At the end of the list, Leonardo mentioned that he could paint as well as anyone.

Eventually, Leonardo got the job and worked for Sforza for seventeen years. Later he visited other towns and cities in Italy and even visited the king of France. However, he was most greatly honored in Florence and spent much of his career there.

Leonardo always carried a notebook. You would find it difficult to read because he wrote backwards—perhaps as a kind of code. (It was easy

People and Terms to Know

lute—musical instrument like a guitar.

for him to do this because he was left-handed.) To read his notes, you have to look at them in a mirror.

Leonardo's notebooks show that he was interested in everything. His music led him to study sound. He saw a total **eclipse** of the sun and invented a simple way to look at it without hurting his eyes. He said that the sun did not move around the earth, as people believed. His drawings of people led him to the study of the human body. He learned to **dissect** dead bodies. His study of the muscles and the tendons under the skin helped his art. His paintings became more realistic. He also made medical discoveries. He designed sewage disposal systems, pageants for entertainment, a water-powered clock. In his notebooks are designs for things that would not be invented until hundreds of years later. There are plans for bicycles, helicopters, tanks, a parachute, a submarine, and much more.

In his notebooks are designs for things that would be not be invented until hundreds of years later.

People and Terms to Know

eclipse—as an observer sees it, the darkening of one heavenly body, such as the moon, by the shadow of another.

dissect—to divide into parts for study.

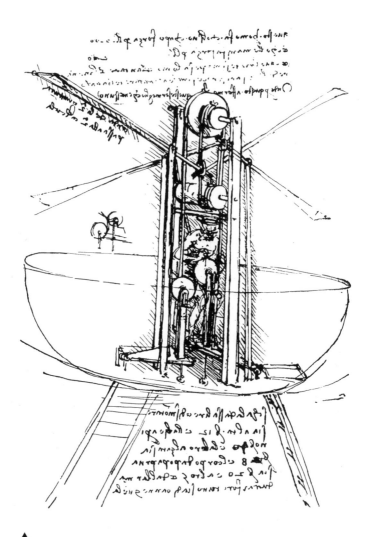

Leonardo's design for a helicopter.

Leonardo learned from observing and experimenting. In this he differed from other people of his time. They read copies of old Greek, Roman, and Egyptian writings and learned from them.

Leonardo said they were using their memories and not their minds.

Leonardo was an explorer of possibilities. In addition to his inventions, he created sculptures, architectural studies and drawings, anatomical studies, and model books on the theory of mechanics. His *Annunciation*, his portraits of Christ and the disciples in *The Last Supper*, and the mysterious woman in the *Mona Lisa* are among the most famous paintings in the world.

Leonardo da Vinci continued to explore the world until he died. He felt that "just as iron rusts when not used, so our mind wastes unless it is used."

QUESTIONS TO CONSIDER

1. What difficulties did Leonardo da Vinci have to overcome?

2. Who would you guess was the biggest influence on Leonardo?

3. What jobs today would probably be best learned through the apprentice system?

4. What was unusual about the style and content of Leonardo's notebooks?

5. Why do people call Leonardo a "Renaissance Man," other than the fact that he was born during the Renaissance?

The Apprenticeship System

The medieval associations of craftsmen known as guilds established an apprenticeship system to train workers. Each worker who wanted to practice a craft—whether it was baking bread or painting pictures—had to move through the following stages:

Apprentice A child served as an unpaid apprentice for five to nine years in a master's workshop to learn his trade.

Journeyman When his apprenticeship was over, a young man became a journeyman and could go to work for wages. As a final step in the learning process, a journeyman made an item—whether it was a shoe, a barrel, a sword, or a painting—that qualified as a "masterpiece."

Master A journeyman whose products met guild standards was welcomed into the guild as a master and could train his own apprentices.

Leonardo da Vinci for Kids: His Life and Ideas
by Janis Herbert

Janis Herbert uses text, pictures, and activities to introduce one of the most fascinating people of the Renaissance.

Leonardo da Vinci
by Diane Stanley

Diane Stanley's biography gives a complete account of the life and achievements of Leonardo.

The Second Mrs. Gioconda
by E. L. Konigsburg

E. L. Konigsburg's historical novel explores the mystery behind Leonardo's most famous painting, Mona Lisa.

Sir Thomas More: A Man of Honor

BY STEPHEN FEINSTEIN

The news reached me like a thunderbolt. It plunged me into the deepest, darkest gloom. My dear friend **Sir Thomas More** had just been found guilty of **treason**. He had been given the death sentence! How could such a terrible thing have happened? More was admired and respected as a man of honor. "Is there no longer justice in England?" I wondered.

It was Sir Thomas's sense of honor that had gotten him into this trouble. His honor had stopped him from signing the oath recognizing King Henry VIII as the head of the Church of England.

People and Terms to Know

Sir Thomas More—(1478–1535) English statesman, author of *Utopia*, and Catholic martyr and saint.

treason—high crime of betraying one's country.

Thomas More (left) and his family.

It had all started fifteen months ago. King Henry wanted a divorce. His wife Catherine of Aragon had not had any sons. Now he wanted to marry the young Anne Boleyn. But the Catholic pope in Rome would not approve of the divorce. Sir Thomas More was England's **lord chancellor** and King Henry's friend. Sir Thomas had a reputation for fairness and honesty, and the king wanted his approval. Sir Thomas was a Catholic. He could not approve the divorce. King Henry was furious.

H enry was frustrated. He had set up a new church. He had declared that he, and not the pope, was the Supreme Head of the Church of England. Then he had demanded that everyone take an oath recognizing him as the head of this church.

Most people took the oath, regardless of their true feelings. Why, I myself signed the oath. I decided that these were only words, after all. But Sir Thomas refused the oath.

People and Terms to Know

lord chancellor—high official in England's government, the presiding officer in the House of Lords. Parliament is made up of the House of Lords (nobles and high-ranking church officials) and the House of Commons (common people).

King Henry had Sir Thomas arrested and imprisoned in the grim **Tower of London**. Fifteen months later, he was brought to trial. On the first of July 1535, the jury gave its **verdict**. It had taken them only fifteen minutes to find Sir Thomas guilty of treason. The new lord chancellor sentenced my old friend to death. Sir Thomas's execution was set for July 6.

On July 3, I learned of the death sentence. Perhaps it was hopeless, but I had to do something to try to save him. I quickly packed a few things and had my horse saddled and ready to ride. In the pouring rain, I flew along the road to London at a full gallop. As I traveled, I put together a plan in my mind. I arrived in London in the evening on July 4, soaking wet and spattered with mud. I took a room at an inn along the **Thames**, not far from the Tower. The next day, the rain finally stopped. I moved about the city, making plans with people I knew from the old days.

After dark, I made my way to the Tower of London. What I was about to do was dangerous.

People and Terms to Know

Tower of London—famous prison in London, England.
verdict—judgment, or opinion, about guilt or innocence in a trial.
Thames (tems)—river in southern England that flows through London.

My heart was pounding when the guards at the gate stopped me. If I could not talk them into helping me, I could be arrested. But luck was with me, and soon I was inside the Tower. As I bounded up the stairs, a voice above me cried out, "Who goes there?" Again, I was lucky. The night watchman led me down a dark hall to a cell and unlocked the door.

I entered the cell. There before me in the dim, flickering light of the candles was a man I hardly recognized. He had a long gray beard and was very thin. Could this be my old friend, the man whose lively wit never failed to amuse me? Then I saw the old sparkle in his eyes! Indeed, it was Sir Thomas. Fifteen months in the Tower had aged him terribly. It was cold in the cell. Droplets of water clung to the stone walls. It was a wonder that Sir Thomas had not become seriously ill.

He slowly stood up to greet me. Sir Thomas smiled and addressed me as Master Hugh, just as in the old days. We had become friends when I hired him to represent me in court. Brilliant lawyer that he was, Sir Thomas saved me from losing my land to a powerful neighbor. I swore then that someday I would repay him for helping my family.

Before I could say a word, Sir Thomas threw his arms around me. Then he stood back and looked at me with a raised eyebrow. He asked me how I had managed to get past the guards at the gate.

"You've been locked up for a while, Sir Thomas," I said. "But the world hasn't changed that much. Money still gets things done!"

Why, Sir Thomas asked, had I taken so much trouble to visit him? Now I was going to have to do a lot of fast talking. "Listen, Sir Thomas," I said. "We have little time for talk. Much has been arranged, and we must hurry. Your cell is not locked. The watchman will be looking the other way. It will be the same down at the gate. A boat is waiting at Tower Wharf to take you down the Thames and then across the North Sea to Holland. There, you will be hidden in a safe place. Your wife Alice and the rest of your family will join you later in Holland. Come with me. Now!"

While I was talking, Sir Thomas began to shake his head. My heart sank. I had feared that he might react this way. His daughter Margaret had told me how hard she had tried to persuade her father to take the oath. I don't know why I thought I could persuade him, when his dearest daughter had failed to do so. But I just had to try.

"Sir Thomas," I pleaded, "what good would it do for England to lose a man such as yourself? The world is filled with greedy, lying men whom we could surely do without. But we cannot afford to lose you! Think of the books you have not yet written. Surely the author of <u>Utopia</u> has not given us his final thoughts. If you won't escape with me, please take the oath, for God's sake!"

> *"Surely the author of* Utopia *has not given us his final thoughts."*

Sir Thomas smiled. He patiently explained to me that it was for God's sake that he *didn't* sign the oath. He would be lying if he took the oath. His conscience could not allow this. The world already had more than enough liars, as I had pointed out, without his joining their ranks. He laughed. I marveled that my friend's sense of humor had not left him. I don't know how he felt about going to his execution the next morning. He must have focused beyond pain and agony to the promise of heaven.

I pleaded with him one more time to save himself. But Sir Thomas wouldn't budge. His mind

---

People and Terms to Know

Utopia—Sir Thomas More's literary masterpiece (1516) in which he describes an ideal society. More's book, written in Latin, was widely translated and became very popular throughout Europe. Even today, the word *utopia* means a perfect place.

A map of More's imaginary ideal country, Utopia, from an early copy of his book.

was made up. There was nothing I could do. Sir Thomas felt that running away would bring nothing. He had taken a position on principle. If his life were to mean anything, he had to stand up for what he believed.

We talked a while longer, and then I took my leave. The changing of the guard would come soon. I needed to get out of the Tower of London before the new guards saw me.

The next morning I joined the crowd that had come to Tower Hill to see the execution. King Henry was not present. My heart was heavy. Sir Thomas, looking very frail, climbed up to the **scaffold**. He urged the people to pray for King Henry. He said that he died the king's good servant, but God's first. My eyes filled with tears.

Sir Thomas knelt down and stretched his head on the block. The executioner lifted up his axe.

Suddenly, Sir Thomas signaled the man to wait. I thought he'd had a change of heart and would be saved. Instead, he told the executioner that he would like to remove his beard from the block. He said that the beard, at least, had committed no treason. This was Sir Thomas's last joke. Then the axe fell.

People and Terms to Know

scaffold (SKAF•uhld)—platform that is used in the execution of condemned prisoners. It is where the noose or chopping block is placed.

Later that day, King Henry had an argument with his wife, Anne Boleyn. Already tired of her, he bitterly accused her of causing the death of his good friend Sir Thomas More!

QUESTIONS TO CONSIDER

1. Why did King Henry wish to become head of the Church of England? What is your opinion of his actions?

2. Why was it important to King Henry that Sir Thomas More take the oath?

3. What do you think about Sir Thomas More's actions?

4. If you were asked to sign an oath that went against your beliefs, what would you do?

Sir Thomas More's Utopia

In *Utopia* (1516), Sir Thomas More attacks parts of the society of his time and describes a perfect one. In More's ideal society, all members do as much as they are able to do and get all that they need. More complains that here the idle nobles are rewarded, while common laborers live miserable lives.

What brand of justice is it that any nobleman whatsoever or goldsmith-banker or moneylender... should attain a life of luxury and grandeur on the basis of his idleness or his non-essential work? In the meantime, the common laborer, the wagon driver, the carpenter, and the farmer perform work so hard and continuous that beasts of burden could scarcely endure it and work so essential that no commonwealth could last even one year without it. Yet they earn such scanty fare and lead such a miserable life.

All the World's a Stage

BY WALTER HAZEN

Scene: *The newly restored* <u>*Globe*</u> *theater, which opened in London in 1996.*

Characters:
Richard Throckmorton, Thomas Stuart

[*Enter on stage* Richard Throckmorton, *who bows to the audience.*]

Richard. Good evening, ladies and gentlemen. Let me introduce myself. I am, or I was, Richard Throckmorton. I lived about 400 years ago, so I

People and Terms to Know

Globe—famous London theater where William Shakespeare's plays were performed after 1599. The Globe was pulled down in 1644, after the Puritans closed the theaters. Restoration of the Globe began in 1987.

Shakespeare's Globe Theater during his lifetime.

am a ghost. But do not be alarmed. We ghosts are quite harmless, you know. Stuart and I are here to tell you about the Globe and the playwright who made this theater great: **William Shakespeare**. We all belonged to the same acting company. At first, it was called the Lord Chamberlain's Men, later the King's Men. This was because King **James I** liked us and encouraged our performances. [*Turns and looks into the wings.*] Ah, here is Thomas Stuart.

[Thomas Stuart *enters the stage, stumbles, and falls flat on his face. He laughs, straightens his clothing, and bows to the audience.*]

Thomas. Pardon my clumsiness, kind people. I played a fool so often in Will's plays that I can't help acting like one, even as a ghost.

Richard. Ah, truer words were never spoken, my friend. After several centuries, a confession!

People and Terms to Know

William Shakespeare—(1564–1616) English poet, playwright, and actor considered by many to be the greatest dramatist of all time.
James I—(1566–1625) king of England (1603–1625). James I was the first Stuart king of England and the first to rule both England and Scotland. He became king upon the death of Elizabeth I.

Thomas [*pretending anger and rushing over to* Richard *with a make-believe sword drawn*]. Pray, I think I detect an insult. For that, prepare to meet your Maker!

[*The two rush back and forth several times across the stage, thrusting at each other with make-believe swords and laughing merrily.*]

Richard [*coming to a stop and panting*]. Enough tomfoolery, Tom. Let us not forget why we are here. Now, where should we begin our story?

Thomas. 'Tis best, I think, to begin at the beginning.

Richard [*to the audience and pointing toward* Thomas]. There, my friends, stands a genius!

Thomas [*pretending another sword stab at* Richard]. You know very well what I mean by "the beginning"—when the Globe theater opened in 1599. Will wrote two of his greatest plays that year—*Julius Caesar* and *As You Like It*.

People and Terms to Know

Julius Caesar and *As You Like It*—two of Shakespeare's plays first performed in 1599–1600. *Julius Caesar* is a tragedy, *As You Like It* a comedy.

Richard. Yes, but he had already written eighteen plays before the Globe opened. He was writing and acting at The Theatre then.

Thomas [*to the audience*]. Yes. The Globe was built years after The Theatre, which opened in London in 1576. Will began writing and acting there in about 1589, if I recall correctly. The Theatre was England's first playhouse.

Richard. Yes, and, for a few years, it was a great success. But in 1597, its lease ran out and the property owners would not renew it. [*Makes an imaginary stab with his sword, aimed at the property owner in question.*] But did the Burbage brothers, who owned The Theatre, give up? No! They had the building taken apart board by board and floated across the Thames River to another lot, where it was put together again. What a task!

Thomas. This ghost can't help sweating, just thinking about the work that took!

Richard. You're a nincompoop, Tom! Ghosts do not sweat!

Thomas [*gasping for air*]. Ah, but we pant heavily!

Richard. On with our story! [*Again faces the audience.*] Once The Theatre was put back together, it was given a new name. In Shakespeare's *As You Like It,* one character says, "All the world's a stage." Because we actors felt the same, we called the rebuilt theater the Globe. It was there that Will wrote and acted in some of the greatest plays ever written. <u>*Hamlet*</u>! Ah, there was a part for a ghost! [*He pretends to pull a cloak about him. He points a shaking finger and adopts a quavering voice.*] "Revenge! Revenge!"

Thomas. Don't forget <u>*Macbeth*</u>, Richard! Ah, what terrifying poetry Will wrote for those witches, the Weird Sisters! There were three of them and there are only two of us, but let's try it! [*Bends over, pretending to be a witch.*] "When shall we three meet again? In thunder, lightning, or in rain?"

Richard [*also pretending to be a witch. The two pretend to stir a large boiling pot.*]. "Round about the cauldron go; in the poisoned entrails throw. First boil in the charmed pot, a toad that poisonous venom's got!" [*The two dance around the cauldron.*]

People and Terms to Know

Hamlet—play by Shakespeare in which a Danish prince is urged by the ghost of his murdered father to get revenge.

Macbeth—play by Shakespeare in which a Scottish nobleman decides to murder his king because three witches say he will be the next king.

Ingredients for a Witch's Brew

1 cauldron—large cooking pot

entrails—intestines, animals' guts

a toad full of venom (poison)

a slice (fillet) of a snake from the bog (fen)

a lizard's eye (eye of newt)

a frog's toe

a bat's skin (wool)

a dog's tongue

and many other ghastly things

Brew a long time.

Chant magic songs over it.

Richard and Thomas. "Double, double, toil and trouble; fire burn and cauldron bubble."

Thomas. "Fillet of a fenny snake, in the cauldron boil and bake; eye of newt and toe of frog, wool of bat, and tongue of dog. . . ." [*Breathes deeply, and then stands up.*]

Richard [*as himself*]. Will even scared his actors with those lines! Ah, the Globe! What pleasant memories.

Thomas. And what of the audience? They were an interesting lot!

Richard. My favorites were the "groundlings." They paid a penny to watch the play from the ground in the yard. If it rained, they got soaked. Remember, they often got rowdy!

Thomas. Aye, even in fair weather, they could get unruly. How many times were we pelted with apples and pears if they didn't like a play? [*Laughs, and playfully thrusts at* Richard *with his sword.*] I remember that you once caught two or three kinds of fruit right between the eyes!

Richard [*playfully returning the sword thrusts*]. I remember you trying to say your lines with several eggs running down your face!

Thomas [*to the audience*]. Not everyone stood on the ground to watch the plays. Those who paid more sat in the roofed sections of the theater. And those who paid the most sat in the Lords' Rooms. Queen Elizabeth sat there!

Richard [*turning to* Thomas]. Speaking of the Lords' Rooms, do you remember the day the Globe burned down? One gentleman's pants caught on fire and a quick-thinking fellow doused his trousers with a mug of ale!

[Thomas *dashes across the stage, holding the seat of his pants and yelling loudly, followed by* Richard, *who pretends to throw a mug of ale on the flames.*]

Thomas. Thank you, Richard. I needed that!

Richard [*to the audience*]. We succeeded because of the great plays that Will wrote. Most years, he

▲
The interior of a theater of Shakespeare's time.

wrote two new plays for us to act in. Some were tragedies, some were comedies, and some were histories. In a tragedy, the hero is brought to ruin or terrible sorrow. Will wrote many famous tragedies. We performed two of his greatest, *King Lear* and *Macbeth*, in a single season, 1605–1606.

Thomas. Don't forget the comedies! The groundlings always loved Will's comedies, with their jokes, wordplay, and happy endings. Will wrote fourteen comedies. My favorites were ___A Midsummer Night's Dream___ and ___Twelfth Night___.

Richard. But Will could write anything, anything! He wrote 37 plays in all, even history plays about the lives of English kings and Roman emperors. Remember **Richard III**? [*He bends over, walks as if he had a hunchback, and looks over his shoulder with an evil look.*]

People and Terms to Know

A Midsummer Night's Dream and *Twelfth Night*—two of Shakespeare's most famous comedies. *A Midsummer Night's Dream* is about two pairs of mismatched lovers. It was first performed during the 1595–1596 season. *Twelfth Night* is about a girl who disguises herself as boy and becomes the servant of a duke with whom she falls in love. It was first performed in 1601–1602.

Richard III—(1452–1485) English king believed to have had two young princes murdered in order to gain the throne. Shakespeare presented him as an evil hunchback in his play *Richard III*.

Thomas. Will just couldn't help writing. He scribbled all the time. Will wrote 159 poems, too. They were beautiful! "Shall I compare thee to a summer's day? Thou art more lovely and more temperate: Rough winds do shake the darling buds of

_____

"Shall I compare thee to a summer's day?"

_____

May and summer's lease hath all too short a date. . . ." Will helped shape English into the wonderful language it is today.

Richard. Dear friends, our time is up. We bid you good-bye and return to the world of ghosts. But please know that our friend, William Shakespeare, is with you tonight. You could have no greater companion.

QUESTIONS TO CONSIDER

1. What were the main events in the Globe Theater's history?

2. What did you learn from this selection about audiences during Shakespeare's time?

3. What can you tell about Shakespeare's plays from the things Richard and Thomas say and do?

4. Why do you think that people still consider William Shakespeare one of the world's greatest writers?

William Shakespeare & the Globe
by Aliki

Aliki tells two stories—one old and one modern. The first story is that of playwright William Shakespeare and the Globe theater for which he wrote many of his greatest plays. The second is that of American actor Sam Wanamaker and his dream to rebuild Shakespeare's Globe on its original London site.

Shakespeare's Theatre
by Jacqueline Morley

Jacqueline Morley presents an account of Shakespeare's Globe theater and the performances that took place there.

Othello
by Julius Lester

Julius Lester's historical novel is based on one of Shakespeare's greatest plays, Othello.

Artemisia Gentileschi

BY BARBARA LITTMAN

She painted the date "1610" just after her name. Then she leaned back to read what she had just added to her finished painting, *Susanna and the Elders:* "<u>Artemisia Gentileschi</u> 1610."

Artemisia was young, and this was her first major painting. Good painters in her day signed their works, and she was a good painter. "Artemisia Gentileschi"—she liked the way that looked. Artemisia was used to seeing "Orazio Gentileschi"

People and Terms to Know

Artemisia Gentileschi (ahr•tuh•MEE•zhuh ɟEHN•tee•LEHS•kee)— (1593–c. 1653) Italian painter. Gentileschi was one of the followers of the famous painter Caravaggio.

Self-portrait by Artemisia Gentileschi.

on paintings. Orazio was her father and a very successful **Baroque** painter.

Gentileschi had grown up surrounded by her father's work. Painters, apprentices, and models filled her father's studio every day. She had watched as models were dressed and positioned. She saw how the painters took measurements and made mathematical calculations. She looked over their shoulders as they calculated the correct **perspective**. She saw

Painters had to learn mathematics, geometry, anatomy, and perspective.

them draw in horizon lines and **vanishing points**. To make paintings look real, painters had to learn mathematics, geometry, anatomy, and perspective.

Artemisia also watched as the apprentices mixed paints. She saw them prepare the clear varnish that went over finished paintings. All of the apprentices eventually got to paint. At first, they

---

People and Terms to Know

Baroque (buh•ROHK)—style in art and architecture in Europe from about 1550 to 1700. Baroque painting stressed realism, movement, and emotion. Baroque painters used real people as models. Bright colors and intense shadows gave drama to their paintings.

perspective—in painting, the use of lines and shading to give the impression of three dimensions on a flat, or two-dimensional, surface. See the painting on page 12.

vanishing points—points at which parallel lines drawn in perspective seem to meet. Artists use vanishing points to create the effect of distance in their works.

painted small details only. Her father or another master painter would check on them regularly. As their work got better, they were allowed to paint more important parts of the painting.

Artemisia got to know many good painters who were her father's friends. One of these, **Michelangelo Caravaggio**, was famous. He was a little wild and had even been to prison for fighting. But his paintings were interesting and beautiful. Unlike many of the painters before him, he painted in a very realistic style. He used real working people as models. He also looked at real animals and the landscape when he sketched or painted. And he didn't use dark outlines to show shapes. Instead, he used different shades and colors of light and dark paint to make objects and people look as they did in real life.

Eventually, paintings done in Caravaggio's realistic style became very popular. **Art patrons** paid well for them. Artemesia would later use the realistic style in her own paintings.

People and Terms to Know

Michelangelo Caravaggio (kar•uh•VAH•joh)—(1571–1610) Italian painter who had many followers among other painters.

Art patrons—wealthy people who supported artists by commissioning (ordering or buying) works from them.

Artemisia was lucky to be Orazio Gentileschi's daughter. She was a natural artist, with a good eye for colors and shapes. In Renaissance Italy, girls were not allowed to become painters' apprentices. Fortunately, her father recognized her talent and encouraged it. He arranged private lessons for her.

Artemisia was only 17 in 1610 when she signed her first major painting. This painting was so good that many didn't believe it was hers. They thought her father had painted it and let her sign it.

Artemisia Gentileschi continued to paint even though many people disapproved of her. Her work was good, even when she was young. Many patrons, including the wealthy Medici family who ruled Florence, ordered artwork from her.

Gentileschi's talent and skill allowed her a way of life unknown to most other women of her time. She could earn money, travel, and meet interesting people.

In 1614, Gentileschi moved to Florence with her husband, who was also a painter. There she became friends with the famous scientist **Galileo**.

People and Terms to Know

Galileo (gal•luh•LAY•oh)—Galileo Galilei (1564–1642), Italian astronomer, mathematician, and physicist. His work formed the foundation of modern experimental science.

◀ This is one of several paintings Artemisia Gentileschi did of the biblical heroine Judith and her maidservant.

The Buonarotis—the family of the famous painter **Michelangelo**—ordered a painting from her. She also had other important commissions. When she was only 23, the Academy of Design in Florence made her a member.

For the next fifteen years or so, Gentileschi lived in the Italian cities of Genoa, Rome, Venice,

People and Terms to Know

Michelangelo (mih·kuhl·AN·juh·loh)—(1475–1564) one of the greatest artists in world history. Among his works are the paintings on the Sistine Chapel in Rome and statues of David and Moses.

and Naples. Her paintings were in demand. In 1625, while in Rome, she painted *Judith and Her Maidservant with the Head of Holofernes.* Based on a story from the Bible, it shows Judith and her maidservant as two strong women. They went to the battlefront to kill the Babylonian general Holofernes before he could invade their village.

This painting has the rich colors, deep shadows, and realistic people that Gentileschi learned from Caravaggio. She used these things to express her personal vision of female heroism.

Gentileschi drew herself in a pose unusual for a woman of her time: painting!

Many of Gentileschi's paintings show powerful women. She painted Minerva, the goddess of wisdom and war, and Cleopatra, the queen of Egypt. She also painted Clio, a goddess of the arts, and St. Catherine. In her self-portrait, Gentileschi drew herself in a pose unusual for a woman of her time: painting!

In 1638, Gentileschi's skill led her to England. There she and her father lived in the court of King Charles I. Together they painted the ceiling of the

Queen's House in Greenwich. Though Artemisia and her father had not been friendly much of her life, now he was 76 years old. He needed her talent and energy. Together, father and daughter painted nine paintings showing how King Charles I supported the arts.

Gentileschi returned to Italy and settled in Naples. There she found a good patron who supported her and her work until her death in 1653.

QUESTIONS TO CONSIDER

1. How would you describe the realistic style that Gentileschi used in her paintings?

2. What kinds of things did painters in the Renaissance need to know to be successful?

3. How was it important to Gentileschi's career that her father approved of her work?

4. In what ways was Gentileschi's life unique for a woman of her time?

Antonio's Apprenticeship:
Painting a Fresco in Renaissance Italy
by Taylor Morrison

*Through the eyes of Antonio, a young apprentice,
Taylor Morrison presents a picture of a typical
artist's studio in Florence in the 1400s.*

Outrageous Women of the Renaissance
by Vicki León

*Vicki León tells the stories of a number of extraor-
dinary women of the Renaissance, including Italian
painter Elisabetta Sirani, who opened an all-female
art school and became an international sensation.*

Renaissance Art:
The Invention of Perspective
by Lillo Canta

*Lillo Canta describes the various methods used
by Renaissance artists to give realistic depth to
their paintings.*

The World
Expands

Silk Road
from China

BY JUDITH LLOYD YERO

$\mathbf{M}$y name is Song Chau. I begin this journal because today my friends and I leave the Chinese capital of Cambuluc. We are beginning what will surely be the most difficult but rewarding journey of our lives. Some would call me an adventurer. However, I am going because I will learn so much about the world outside of my Chinese homeland. We will travel the **Silk Road** in the footsteps of great traders and explorers like **Xuan Huang** and the westerner **Marco Polo**.

People and Terms to Know

Silk Road—system of ancient caravan routes across Central Asia, along which traders carried silk and other goods.

Xuan Huang (SHOO•wen HWANG)—Chinese Buddhist monk who traveled the Silk Road from 629 to 644. He brought back Buddhist scriptures from India and spent the rest of his life translating them.

Marco Polo—(1254–1324) Italian merchant and traveler from Venice who traveled along the Silk Road to Asia. He spent many years with the Mongol emperor of China, Kublai Khan. When he returned to Europe, he wrote about his travels.

aquesta caravana es
de sarra ...

los ... ...

c ...

A camel caravan travels on the Silk Road.

This is an exciting time to be young and adventurous. The great emperor **Kublai Khan** encourages poetry, art, and trade of all kinds. Walking the streets of the city is a living lesson in foreign language and customs. Thick-bearded merchants from Central Asia sell wine from goatskin bags. Men in leopard-skin hats and tight-sleeved robes argue the price of goods. Yellow-haired women shop in the marketplace. Religious pilgrims from India wander the streets in sandals. Strange foods fill the marketplace—spinach, garlic, mustard, peas, and delicious-smelling spices brought from lands to the west. I stop at a booth for my favorite little cakes fried in oil and covered with sesame seeds. I will miss these sights and sounds. I am eager to see the places these foreigners come from.

Our last stop before leaving the city is a silk shop. Our **caravan** will take silk to trade for supplies along the way. As I enter the shop, a sound like falling rain fills the air. The shop owner explains that it is the sound of silkworms munching

---

People and Terms to Know

Kublai Khan (KOO•bly KAHN)—(1215–1294) Mongol emperor of China, which had been conquered by his grandfather, Genghis Khan. Kublai Khan built his capital at Cambuluc, near today's Beijing.

caravan—group of travelers or traders traveling cross-country with pack animals.

mulberry leaves. This sound has been heard only in China for 3,000 years! For most of that time, only we Chinese knew this secret of making silk.

Foreigners said silk was made of the fuzz scraped from the leaves of mulberry trees. How foolish! It showed we kept our secret well.

Emperors once ordered death to anyone who told the secret or secretly took silkworms to foreign lands. Many have tried, and unfortunately some have succeeded. Women have hidden the silkworm eggs in their fancy hairdos. Men have put them into hollow bamboo poles used as walking sticks.

Emperors once ordered death to anyone who told the secret or secretly took silkworms to foreign lands.

The silkworm eats, spins its cocoon, and is killed. Its silken cocoon is unwound by women with sharp eyes and great patience. They spin the tiny strands into fine, but strong threads. The cloth spun from these threads is famous for its beauty and softness. It is prized throughout the known world. Other lands now know the secret. But their silk is never as fine as that made in China.

We soon will travel to the West. The way to the West is like the spidery threads of the silkworm. Paths worn by the feet of camels, horses, and men weave across the dry landscape. Each path seeks an easier route across oceans of stones and towering mountains. For hundreds of years, people like us have traveled these paths. We trade the silk and other fine goods made only in China. In exchange, we receive treasures produced only in the West.

Traveling to the West once had other dangers. Bandits and thieves attacked the caravans. Our great khan now protects all who travel this route. My friends and I can only shudder to think of what our ancestors went through in earlier **dynasties**.

Many weeks of travel have left us weary. Fortunately, stories of earlier travelers helped us to prepare. We learned that when we cross a deep river, we must build a raft. We fill a bag sewn from many goatskins with air. We tie the raft on top of the bag. This makes the raft ride high, even when

People and Terms to Know

dynasties—successions of rulers who belong to the same family. Used this way, the word means "eras" or "times."

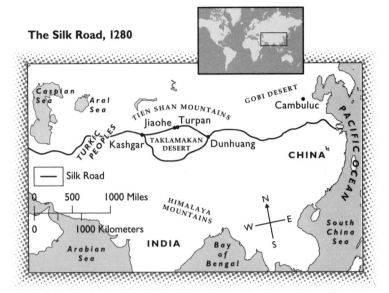

The Silk Road, 1280

Caspian Sea

Aral Sea

TIEN SHAN MOUNTAINS

GOBI DESERT

Cambuluc

Jiaohe Turpan

TURKIC PEOPLES

Kashgar TAKLAMAKAN DESERT Dunhuang

CHINA

PACIFIC OCEAN

— Silk Road

0   500   1000 Miles

0   1000 Kilometers

HIMALAYA MOUNTAINS

N

W   E

S

INDIA

Bay of Bengal

South China Sea

Arabian Sea

loaded with our camels and supplies. It's not easy to get the camels aboard without tipping the raft. We dry quickly in the heat!

At last, our first great reward is in sight. Dunhuang! Hundreds of caves pierce a cliff face that stretches as far as I can see. These caves were dug by monks and others wishing to honor the **Buddha** or to leave an offering. Artists have covered the walls of these caves with colorful wall paintings and silk hangings.

We approach with great excitement. First, we enter a cool, dark cave. The flicker of flames draws me forward toward a narrow doorway. When

People and Terms to Know

Buddha (BOO•duh)—(563–483 B.C.) Indian philosopher and founder of Buddhism. His real name was Siddhartha Gautama. *Buddha* means "Enlightened One."

I step through, I am struck dumb. My eyes travel upward to view a huge statue of the Buddha. His head rises above me to the height of 15 men. The Buddha's hand is raised in a position that says, "Do not be afraid."

We rest here. Tomorrow we begin an even more difficult journey.

* * *

Taklamakan is the great desert whose name means "go in and you will not come out." We have traveled its edge for days. Now we see what looks like a thin line of trees in the distance. This could mean water, at last!

> *Taklamakan is the great desert whose name means "go in and you will not come out."*

The **oasis** of Turpan has the hottest summer days in all of China. But it is blessed with the one thing that every desert traveler prizes above all things—water. This gift comes from the Tien Shan, mountains in the north that are always capped with snow. The water reaching Turpan makes the land green and beautiful. Grape arbors cover the streets

---

People and Terms to Know

oasis (oh•AY•sis)—fertile or green spot in a desert or wasteland.

in the town, and cotton grows in the fields. My friends and I feast hungrily on melons and grapes of every color.

In the town of Jiaohe, we feel that we have returned home. This is one of the central markets for those who do not wish to travel the full distance from the East or the West. Here, caravan leaders bargain for rich goods seen nowhere else. They offer medicines, perfumes, wines, spices, fragrant woods, books, and woven rugs. There are animals we have never before seen. We see peacocks, parrots, small, swift antelopes known as gazelles, falcons, lions, and the one they call the camel bird—the ostrich.

We will spend a few days here, renewing our strength.

* * *

A few days ago, we reached the **Turkic lands** of the West. The greatest interest here, of course, is the "heavenly horses." They are magnificent beasts with lean bodies and long legs and necks.

People and Terms to Know

Turkic lands—region east of the Caspian Sea, inhabited by peoples speaking one of the Turkic family of languages.

Their riders cover them in felt blankets and layers of silk. Jeweled bands around their necks make these beasts appear like the emperor himself. We understand now why one of the **Tang** emperors sent men and caravans loaded with silk to find and purchase horses for his court.

*   *   *

We have done very well in our trading. We have some silk left, so we will continue on. Perhaps we will even cross the sea that leads to the great cities of Europe. If not, I have already stored enough wonders in my memory to last a lifetime.

QUESTIONS TO CONSIDER

1. Why were the streets of Cambuluc a "living lesson in foreign language and customs"?

2. Why do you think the Silk Road had so many different paths?

3. Why do you think that early Chinese emperors threatened people with death for telling foreigners the secret of how silk was made?

4. What part of the trip on the Silk Road would have been your favorite if you had been part of the caravan? Why?

People and Terms to Know

Tang—dynasty in China that ruled from 681 to 907.

Stories from the Silk Road
by Cherry Gilchrist

Cherry Gilchrist takes readers for a trip on the Silk Road, stopping to retell stories drawn from the cultures of the peoples that lived along the ancient trade routes from China to Persia.

Made in China: Ideas and Inventions from Ancient China
by Suzanne Williams

Besides producing silk, the ancient Chinese made many contributions to world civilization. Suzanne Williams describes some of the most important.

Marco Polo: A Journey Through China
by Fiona MacDonald

Fiona MacDonald describes the travels of Marco Polo, who journeyed from Venice to China along the Silk Road in the 1270s.

The Daring Portuguese

BY LYNNETTE BRENT

D~ay~ 1

Evening has come. Maybe I can finally get some rest! It's hard work to man the sails, and I am often clumsy. The other men on the <u>caravel</u> can tell I am not an experienced sailor.

We have a very important mission: to sail to <u>Cape Bojador</u> in search of a new way into Africa. <u>Prince Henry</u> planned and paid for our voyage. (I hear that the English call him "The Navigator.")

People and Terms to Know

caravel—small ship with three masts and lateen sails. See page 159. Caravels were used in the 1400s and 1500s.

Cape Bojador (BOH•ha•DOHR)—point of land on Africa's west coast. See the map on page 156. *Bojador* means "bulging cape" in Portuguese.

Prince Henry—(1394–1460) younger brother of Portugal's king. Prince Henry's school for navigators at Sagres near Cape St. Vincent was a center for mapmaking and shipbuilding. The prince sponsored many voyages of discovery.

A caravel.

Our prince is sure that riches can be found in Africa. This voyage could make our nation wealthy. First we have to find a trade route. We must be first! We need to do it before other Europeans settle in the same place.

This voyage could make our nation wealthy. First we have to find a trade route.

Trade is not our only goal. Prince Henry is a religious man. He hopes that we can spread Christianity in the new lands we discover.

For now, I don't care about religion or wealth. I just hope that I can survive the journey.

Day 8

The maps that Prince Henry gave us are in another language. They show lands that the sailors on board have never seen or heard about. Some of the older sailors are grumbling about the new maps. They ask why the maps don't show the places they've heard about for years. But the captain insists that these new maps are correct. Prince Henry found the maps. They belonged to Jewish sailors who were allowed into North Africa long ago. I hope the captain is right. If he isn't, we are headed for completely unknown territory!

All of the sailors are nervous about this trip. They've heard stories. They've heard that the waters around Cape Bojador are very shallow and have dangerous currents. Some people even say that beyond this point the sea boils.

Something else caused trouble between the captain and crew. We found out that the captain has much less experience than most of the sailors on board (except for me). The sailors were very angry about this. This is a dangerous voyage, they say. Still, the captain swears that he will keep us safe, even in these rough waters. His skills in **navigation** are strong. So the crew is obeying his orders, but they are watching him closely.

I work hard to keep up with the other men on deck. I watch the better sailors, and I am getting better at moving the sails and tying all of the knots. I'm still very tired, but I can sleep. Even with the constant movement of the ship and the roll of the waves underneath, I'm not seasick.

People and Terms to Know

navigation—planning, recording, and controlling the course of a ship. A person who does this work is called a navigator.

Day 18

Today a fight broke out on deck. Some of the sailors come from other parts of Europe. They are only here because of the promise of riches and don't care about the Portuguese rulers. Others, like me, are loyal Portuguese. We trust Prince Henry.

Everybody's tired now. This is a long voyage. The foreign sailors are complaining about Prince Henry and call him a coward for not joining us on this trip. It was his idea, they say. He will take credit for this dangerous voyage, but he did nothing but provide us with the plans and the ships.

Today on deck, many of the Portuguese fought to defend the prince's honor. I stayed out of the brawl. Still, I thought hard about what had been said. Prince Henry couldn't possibly have sailed with us. He could be captured by the pirates that sail around North Africa! I know he and his brothers defeated them years ago. They might kill him in revenge! The prince couldn't have lived on our ship, either. It's dirty and crowded and is no place for royalty.

The captain finally stopped the fight. He had the foreign sailors **flogged**. The Portuguese sailors were

People and Terms to Know

flogged—whipped severely. A flogging was a common form of discipline used to control sailors and to punish criminals.

not punished. They had been simply defending the prince's honor. The captain said that this is the last fight he'll stand for on his ship. He told the guards to watch the crew from now on.

Day 35

I am amazed that I am still alive.

After over a month at sea, we were excited about reaching Cape Bojador. The crew had settled down, and our captain was still in command. Even I felt like a seasoned sailor.

Then a storm caught us completely offguard. We were tossed and thrown for so long, I was sure that we would all drown. Finally the storm passed. Our car-

I am amazed that I am still alive.

avel was so badly damaged that we drifted at sea for days. We rationed our food and supplies. We had no idea how long we would be at sea. We all expected to die.

Then something amazing happened. We drifted to an island! Here we found a sheltered area and set up camp. We found enough food to keep us from starving. Now we're repairing our ship. In a few days, we will be ready to set sail again.

It seems like a miracle!

Portuguese Exploration, 1419–1498

PORTUGAL
Lisbon
Cape St. Vincent
Madeira Islands (1418)
Cape Bojador
(1434)

Mediterranean Sea

Cape Verde
Islands
(1444)
SIERRA
LEONE
(1460)

AFRICA

INDIA
(1498)

EQUATOR

ATLANTIC
OCEAN

INDIAN
OCEAN

Cape of
Good Hope
(1487)

N
W — E
S

0   1000   2000 Miles

0   2000 Kilometers

Back in Portugal

We've returned to Portugal safely. Our ship is still damaged, but shipbuilders here will repair it before the next voyage. When we left the ship, the captain told me that I had done a good job. He invited me to go on the next **expedition** to Africa.

People and Terms to Know

expedition—important journey by a group of people taken for a specific purpose.

Back when we were on the island, the captain had decided not to go on to Cape Bojador. It was a good decision. We had fixed the caravel and stocked up on fish and plants from the island, but we couldn't really continue to the Cape. We didn't know exactly where we were. Maybe it would be a long trip. Maybe our supplies wouldn't hold out. It was safer to return home.

We left our island, which we named **Porto Santo**, and headed north. After sailing about 500 miles, we saw Cape St. Vincent again. Finally, here was a landmark we knew! Now we could find our way home.

Prince Henry was disappointed that we never reached Cape Bojador. Still, we came back with maps and experiences that will help us in future voyages. Our next trip will be back to Porto Santo, our safe harbor. There we will build a port that we can use to launch new trips farther down the African coast. Soon Prince Henry will see his dream become reality. Portugal will have a trade route in the heart of Africa.

People and Terms to Know

Porto Santo—(Spanish, "Blessed Port") one of the Madeira Islands.

*   *   *

Between 1418 and 1434, Prince Henry sent fifteen expeditions to try to reach Cape Bojador. Finally, in 1434, Captain Gil Eanes, a squire from Prince Henry's household, accidentally sailed beyond it. When he stepped out on the deserted African shore, he saw that it was not as threatening as the sailors had feared.

Prince Henry's expeditions continued to push south down the African coast. In 1487, Bartolomeu Dias reached Africa's southern tip, the Cape of Good Hope. In 1498, Vasco da Gama sailed around Africa to India. As a result of these explorations, the Portuguese gained a large colonial empire.

QUESTIONS TO CONSIDER

1. What were Prince Henry's goals in sending sailors down Africa's coast?

2. What problems occurred during the voyage? How did the captain cope with them?

3. Why do you think that Prince Henry might have chosen a captain who didn't have much experience?

4. How would you feel about going on a voyage of discovery into unknown regions?

Caravel

Prince Henry the Navigator was eager to explore the world. He planned to send out many expeditions of discovery. Since these voyages would be risky, Henry's sailors needed a new type of ship. The new ships would have to survive long months in open seas and then return home again, sailing into the wind. The ships could be small, but they would need to turn easily.

Prince Henry found some useful features in ships built by the Arabs and the Greeks. Finally, Henry's shipbuilders produced a ship called the caravel. A caravel was about 75 feet long and about 25 feet wide, with two or three lateen sails. These sails were triangular and attached to a short mast. A caravel could hold supplies for a crew of about twenty men, who would sleep on deck, except in bad weather. A famous mariner from Venice called the caravels "the best ships that sailed the seas." Caravels became the standard ship of discovery.

▲
Caravels with lateen sails.

A Long and Uncertain Journey:
The 27,000 Mile Voyage of Vasco da Gama
by Tom McNeely

Tom McNeely tells the story of Vasco Da Gama's epic voyage from Portugal around the southern tip of Africa to India.

Vasco da Gama and
the Portuguese Explorers
by Rebecca Stefoff
(with an introduction by astronaut Michael Collins)

Rebecca Stefoff describes the journeys of the Portuguese explorers who helped establish Portugal's empire in the 1400s and 1500s.

Around the World in a Hundred Years:
From Henry the Navigator to Magellan
by Jean Fritz

Jean Fritz presents biographies of ten major explorers, providing an account of the hundred-year period during which Europeans explored much of the world.

Voyage Around the World

BY MARIANNE McCOMB

The people of Sanlúcar de Barrameda, Spain, waited eagerly for news. A great ship had pulled into harbor the night before, on September 6, 1522. Three years earlier, the *Victoria* had sailed from this port. She was one of five ships commanded by Captain **Ferdinand Magellan**. Was he finally back? Where were the other four ships?

A large crowd gathered at the docks. Eighteen men, the *Victoria*'s crew, made their way off the ship. Many sailors were so weak that they could barely stand. Still, they were eager to tell their story.

People and Terms to Know

Ferdinand Magellan—(c. 1480–1521) Portuguese sailor and navigator, leader of the expedition that was the first to travel completely around the globe.

This world map, made in the 1500s, a few years after Magellan's voyage,

* * *

The story these sailors told was an incredible one. On September 20, 1519, Magellan and a crew of nearly 270 men had sailed off in five huge ships: the *Trinidad*, *San Antonio*, *Concepción*, *Victoria*, and *Santiago*. Spirits ran high on the day they sailed out of port. King **Charles V** himself had approved Magellan's voyage. Magellan's mission was to prove that at least a part of the wealth-giving **Moluccas Islands** lay within Spanish territory. If he was right, the Portuguese, who controlled trade to the Moluccas, would have to let Spain share in the profitable spice business.

To prove his theory, Magellan had to find a new, all-Spanish route to the Moluccas. The Portuguese controlled the usual route east around Africa and across the Indian Ocean to the **South Sea**. Magellan had promised King Charles that he had a different route in his mind. He would sail westward across the Atlantic and find a new passageway around or through the land then called Tierre Firme (today's

---

People and Terms to Know

Charles V—(1500–1558) greatest of the Hapsburg emperors. He ruled over a vast empire that included Belgium, the Netherlands, Austria, Spain, and the Spanish lands in the Americas.

Moluccas (muh•LUHK•uhz) **Islands**—name for the Spice Islands, a group of islands in eastern Indonesia.

South Sea—former name for the Pacific Ocean.

Voyage Around the World   163

South America). When he found the passageway, Magellan said, he would continue sailing west across the South Sea to the Moluccas.

King Charles agreed to pay for the trip. Magellan quickly put together a fleet and gave the order to set sail.

The first part of Magellan's voyage—across the Atlantic—was uneventful. In early December, the five ships reached Rio de Janeiro. After docking, Magellan sent a series of expeditions up and down the coast of South America. He told his men to search for a waterway through the continent to the South Sea.

Soon the weather grew stormy and cold. Magellan stopped the expeditions. For the next five months, Magellan's fleet was stuck in the port of San Julián. Angry, his crew staged a **mutiny** against him. Two Spanish officers and a group of sailors tried to take control of the fleet. The officers were jealous of Magellan's skills and annoyed because he was Portuguese. Magellan put down the mutiny very firmly. He executed one of the Spanish officers and abandoned the other onshore at San Julián.

People and Terms to Know

mutiny (MYOO•tin•ee)—revolt of a ship's crew against their captain.

The mutiny only made Magellan more eager to discover the waterway. In August 1520, he once again sent expeditions up and down the coast. On one such expedition, the *Santiago* was dashed against the rocks, and all her men were drowned.

Eventually, far down the coast of the continent, Magellan's crew found a large **inlet**. At the base of the inlet was a narrow waterway. Magellan's men begged him not to go further, but Magellan stood firm. He ordered his two largest ships to follow the waterway.

Magellan and the rest of the crew nervously waited nearby. Many sailors feared that the ships would be wrecked. Finally, however, they sailed back into view. The ships had passed through two bays, and then the men had spotted a narrow **strait** to a third bay beyond. Magellan listened carefully to their description of the strait. Could it lead to the South Sea?

Magellan ordered all four ships to pull up anchor. They made their way into the inlet, following the newly found route. Very soon after starting,

People and Terms to Know

inlet—small or narrow body of water, like a bay or a cove.
strait—narrow channel that connects two bodies of water.

however, the fleet ran into trouble. The waterways the ships were sailing through were incredibly narrow and twisting. On both sides were icy rocks that threatened to wreck the ships. The men were terrified and begged Magellan to turn back. When

The men were terrified and begged Magellan to turn back.

he refused, the crew of the *San Antonio* mutinied and left for Spain. Magellan and his crew watched helplessly as she sailed away, carrying many of the fleet's supplies. Angry and even more determined, Magellan ordered the three remaining ships to sail on.

Many more days passed. The crew became more and more frightened. At last, on November 28, 1520, the *Trinidad, Concepción*, and *Victoria* passed through one final waterway and spotted the magnificent South Sea. When Captain Magellan saw the calm blue waters of the huge ocean, he sank to his knees and cried with joy.

Magellan's relief was short-lived, however. Although sailing was smooth and peaceful on the South Sea, the crew suffered terribly from a lack of food and fresh water. Magellan ignored the sailors' pleas to turn back. They would continue on to the Moluccas, he said, even if it meant eating the rigging—the masts, lines, and sails.

Ferdinand Magellan.

Week after week passed, and still the three boats sailed on. Eventually, the drinking water on the boats turned a strange yellow color and took on a terrible smell. Even so, the men drank their rations greedily. Some of the crew began roasting rats over the fire for food.

Eventually, all of the sailors began to suffer from the swollen, blackened gums of scurvy, a disease caused by lack of vitamin C. The food on the ships was long gone. The men began eating sawdust and leather wrappings from the sails. Magellan's prediction had come true.

By the end of February 1521, the sailors were too weak to raise and lower the sails. The ships simply drifted where the wind took them. A desperate Magellan tried to boost his men's spirits. He promised that they would see land soon. Once again, Magellan was right. On March 6, the men heard a hoarse cry from the lookout: "Praise God! Praise God! Land! Land! Land!"

*   *   *

The island that Magellan and his crew had spotted was not one of the Moluccas. Still, they were overjoyed. The three ships headed for the island (today's Guam), and the men made their way to shore. For the first time in 99 days, they had fresh food to eat and fresh water to drink. They bargained for supplies with the natives and slowly began restocking their ships.

On March 9, the three ships left the safety of their island and sailed southwest to Cebu Island in the Philippines. Once again, they dropped anchor and went ashore to gather supplies.

While on Cebu, Magellan converted some of the natives to Christianity. One of his converts was Humabon, a ruler of Cebu. Humabon asked for Magellan's help in attacking the nearby island of Mactan. Magellan agreed. Late in April, Magellan and his sailors tried to land on Mactan. A large group of Mactan natives met them, under the command of a chieftain named **Lapulapu**. A bloody battle followed. Captain Magellan and many of his sailors were killed.

The rest of Magellan's crew was horrified. Their leader was gone! How would they make it home alive? Juan Sebastián del Cano, the captain of the *Concepción*, took over. He ordered the *Concepción's* crew to leave their ship behind. They would continue on with only the *Victoria* and the *Trinidad*.

People and Terms to Know

Lapulapu—(c. 1490–c. 1560) Filipino chieftain now considered a national hero because he prevented the first European invasion of the Philippines.

Eventually del Cano and his men reached the Moluccas. There they took on a cargo of cloves and began the long return voyage to Spain. Along the way, the Portuguese captured the *Trinidad* and imprisoned its crew. Only one ship was left—the *Victoria*.

On September 6, 1522, del Cano and his crew of seventeen men reached Sanlúcar de Barrameda in Spain. Magellan's fleet had finally come home. The men had successfully **circumnavigated** the globe.

QUESTIONS TO CONSIDER

1. What were the key events in Magellan's crew's journey around the world?

2. What were some of the hardships that Magellan and his crew faced during their voyage?

3. How would you describe Magellan?

4. If you had been one of Magellan's crew, how do you think you would have reacted during the voyage?

5. What would you say was Magellan's most important contribution to the world? Why?

People and Terms to Know

circumnavigated—completely circled.

The Dragon and the Spanish Armada

BY SHARON FRANKLIN

"**M**other, may I ask you some questions about Father and the Spanish Armada? We haven't talked about this since I was a boy."

"Oh, yes. All right, Edwin. Let me light the fire first."

The English woman lit the fire and sat with her son, staring at the flames. She thought about her husband and the English navy's battle with the Spanish Armada many years before, in 1588. Her husband had been so proud when he set off to sea. She had mended a small tear in his white leggings and sewed a missing button on his gold-covered vest. He had looked so handsome. Their son, Edwin, home from school on holiday, now was as tall as his father.

A warship of the Spanish Armada blows up after being attacked by

"Edwin, you'll remember that **Sir Francis Drake** and his men—your father with them—were anchored in Plymouth harbor on the 19th of July. Their supplies were being loaded. They were dangerously low on food, and the men had been on half-rations for some time. Your father was keeping watch. That afternoon, the captain of the *Golden Hind* had delivered bad news. The Spanish Armada was sailing directly toward Plymouth, England.

"Your father spotted the fleet when it first appeared on the horizon. More and more ships crept slowly, like giants, into view. The men were terrified. More than 130 enemy ships were heading directly toward them! The English had only about 40 ships. And the wind and the tide were against us."

Edwin sat up straight. "Where was Drake's *Revenge*? What did you say that Drake did?"

People and Terms to Know

Sir Francis Drake—(c. 1540–1596) English admiral and naval hero. Drake earned wealth and popularity by sailing around the world and by making daring raids on Spanish ships.

Golden Hind—only ship of Sir Francis Drake's fleet that survived to successfully circumnavigate the world in 1577–1580.

Revenge—Sir Francis Drake's flagship. A flagship carries the fleet commander and displays his flag.

"The *Revenge* was anchored in Plymouth harbor. As the Spanish ships got closer, our men saw that they had many more cannons than we did. If the Spanish got close enough, they could fire at our ships and then board them.

"An officer raced to tell Vice-Admiral Drake the news. Drake was playing a game of **bowls** near the water's edge. We heard that Drake slowly looked up from the game and then turned calmly back to it. He said that first he would finish his game and then they would beat the Spanish. Drake was very confident. It inspired everyone who sailed with him, including your father."

The young man interrupted. "What did the Spanish used to call Drake?"

"The Spanish were afraid of him. They called him *El Draque,* which means 'The Dragon.' To them, Drake was bigger and more powerful than life."

"Didn't you tell me that Drake often raided their ships?" asked Edwin.

People and Terms to Know

bowls—popular game in England since the 1100s, played on a lawn, or "green." Lopsided balls called bowls are rolled at a smaller target ball.

Queen Elizabeth appears on a medal made to celebrate England's victory over the Armada.

"Yes. For years, Drake had been surprising Spanish ships every chance he got. He even raided them in their own harbors and in their ports in the New World. Then he took all the riches he found on board. These raids made him rich and famous. Queen Elizabeth and Drake worked together against Spain. She supplied him with money and ships. In return, he shared the treasures he brought back with her. You and I got some of them, too."

She opened a drawer and pulled out a handful of coins. "Do you remember? Your father brought these Spanish coins back in 1580. He'd been gone for three years, sailing around the world with Drake in the *Golden Hind*."

"Mother, why did the Spanish send the Armada in the first place?"

"The Spanish, and especially King Philip II, wanted to punish Drake for his raids. Philip wanted to defeat the English once and for all. He assembled these 130 ships—the Spanish Armada—to drive the English from the **English Channel**. Philip thought that this would prove that Spain was the world's most powerful country."

"Then what happened?"

"Luckily for us, Philip had made some important mistakes. He chose an unskilled seaman, the Duke of Medina Sidonia, to command the Armada. The duke knew nothing about planning a naval battle. Drake and Admiral **Howard** were far more experienced and skilled. We also had much better ships. Spanish ships were old, bulky, and hard to control, especially in heavy winds and bad weather. Your father was very proud of the English ships.

People and Terms to Know

English Channel—arm of the Atlantic Ocean between western France and southern England. The English Channel opens into the North Sea. See the map on page 16.

Howard—Charles Howard (1536–1624), first earl of Nottingham. Lord Howard was lord high admiral of the English fleet that fought the Spanish Armada.

They were smaller, longer, and faster, with a better hull design. They were easier to control and could stay on course better in bad weather.

"And so Drake finished his game of bowls, and the battles began. Drake had to invent the battle plans that the English would use. Remember, no naval battle like this one had ever been fought. They also had to battle the weather. Harsh winds, heavy rain, and poor visibility—all were dangerous conditions for men at sea."

"Mother, tell me again about Drake's **fireships**," Edwin said.

"As the Armada got closer, the English kept them moving. Admiral Howard lured them up the English Channel. This went on through July and into August. Finally, on August 7, the Spanish were anchored under the cliffs of Calais, in northern France. Drake believed they were in port to get supplies. He wanted to surprise them. He told Admiral Howard that they should send fireships to sail directly into the sleeping Armada. This would drive the Spanish out of Calais. About eight English merchant ship owners offered their ships to the navy for this purpose.

People and Terms to Know

fireships—English merchant ships that were purposely set on fire and sailed directly into Spanish ships.

"The Spanish dreaded the fireships. They were packed with gunpowder and other explosive items. Each one towed a small boat to help the crew escape at the last moment. The angry sky was ablaze as the fireships moved up to the Armada. The Spanish sailors must have been terrified, watching those burning ships sail directly into them!

The angry sky was ablaze as the fireships moved up to the Armada.

"At first light on August 8, your father saw what had happened the night before. In their panic to escape, some Spanish ships had run into each other. By day's end, the English had damaged more Spanish ships and killed and injured many men. The Spanish tried to escape into the deeper waters of the North Sea, but strong winds helped to spread their ships out and wreck them.

"The English had won! They had destroyed the Spanish Armada! Still, after this battle, the Spanish spread rumors that *they* had won. They spread **broadsides** all over Europe, claiming that they had sunk the *Revenge* and captured Drake. When these

---

People and Terms to Know

broadsides—large sheets of paper printed on one side and used as news bulletins. Broadsides were posted in towns to tell people about important events.

lies reached England, official reports were published. At last the world knew the truth. Spain was defeated, and England had won."

"I wish Father had lived to read those reports," said Edwin.

"So do I, Edwin. But he knew the truth. He was very proud to have helped England defeat Spain's Armada."

"Soon I will be old enough to go to sea myself," said Edwin.

His mother sighed. She hoped that it would not be soon.

QUESTIONS TO CONSIDER

1. What important qualities did Drake possess as a naval leader?

2. What were the most important events in the battle between the English Navy and the Spanish Armada?

3. Why were fireboats a threat to the Spanish?

4. How did the weather affect both English and Spanish sailors?

5. Why do you think control of the English Channel was important to both England and Spain?

Sources

Federigo's Falcon *from Boccaccio's* Decameron *retold by Walter Hazen*

Giovanni Boccaccio lived and wrote in Italy in the 1300s. He is often called the father of Italian prose because of the 100 short stories in his collection, the *Decameron*. The character of Fiammetta, the narrator of "Federigo's Falcon," was based on a woman he admired, a daughter of the king of Naples. The characters in the story are all fictional, but the kind of life described in the story is true in its details to life in his time. Boccaccio's story can be found in the *Decameron* by Giovanni Boccaccio, translated by Guido Waldman with an introduction and notes by Jonathan Usher (New York: Oxford University Press, 1993).

Persecution in Spain *by Barbara Littman*

The narrator, his brother Miguel, and his cousin David are fictional characters. Tomás de Torquemada, Queen Isabella, and King Ferdinand are historical figures. Information provided in the story is historically accurate. Sources include *The Spanish Inquisition* by Cecil Roth, Reader in Jewish Studies at Oxford University (New York: The Norton Library, W. W. Norton & Company, Inc.) and *The Spanish Inquisition, Its Rise, Growth, and End* by Jean Plaidy (New York: The Citadel Press, 1967).

Machiavelli's Advice to Rulers *by Judith Lloyd Yero*

Niccolò Machiavelli, Cesare Borgia, Remirro, and Lorenzo de' Medici are historical figures, and information about them is factually accurate. Direct quotes and descriptions of Machiavelli's ideas are from *The Prince* by Niccolò Machiavelli, edited by W. K. Marriott (London: J. M. Dent and Sons, 1908).

Proper Behavior *by Lynnette Brent*

All the characters in this story are fictional except for the historical figure of Castiglione. Details about the party, the tailor, and how upper-class citizens behaved are historically accurate. *The Book of the Courtier* by Baldassare Castiglione is available in an English translation by George Bull (Hammondsworth, NY: Penguin Books, 1983).

The Six Wives of Henry VIII *by Marianne McComb*

Sir William Gardiner is a fictional character, and no one ever wrote a letter like this to King Henry VIII. The facts it relates, however, are a matter of historical record. More information can be found in *The Six Wives of Henry VIII* by Alison Weir (New York: Grove Weidenfeld, 1992).

Elizabeth I and Her Age *by Stephen Feinstein*

Robert, his parents, and his friend Rupert are fictional characters. The information about Queen Elizabeth and her activities is factually accurate. Sources include *The Public and Private Worlds of Elizabeth I* by Susan Watkins (New York: Thames & Hudson, 1998) and *Queen Elizabeth I* by Betha Zamoyska (New York: McGraw Hill, 1981).

Words into Print *by Stephen Currie*

St. Scholastica monastery and its inhabitants are fictional, but the activities related are based on records of real monasteries. Johann Gutenberg is the historical figure who developed the world's first printing press to use movable type. A good source for information about the impact of printing is *Breaking into Print, Before and After the Invention of the Printing Press* by Stephen Krensky (Boston: Little Brown & Co., 1996).

Renaissance Man *by Dee Masters*

The information about Leonardo da Vinci is factually accurate. Sources include *The Notebooks of Leonardo da Vinci* selected and edited by Irma A. Richter (Oxford; New York: Oxford University Press, 1980), *Leonardo da Vinci, Engineer and Architect* (Montreal: Montreal Museum of Fine Arts 1987), and *Leonardo: Discovering the Life of Leonardo da Vinci* by Serge Bramly, translated by Siân Reynolds (New York: HarperCollins Publishers, 1991).

Sir Thomas More: A Man of Honor *by Stephen Feinstein*

The narrator and his plot to free Sir Thomas More are completely fictional. Information about Thomas More, including his sense of humor and his last words, is factually accurate. Sources include *Statesman and Saint, Cardinal Wolsey, Sir Thomas More, and the Politics of Henry VIII* by Jasper Ridley (New York: The Viking Press, 1983) and *The Life of Sir Thomas More: Humanist as Hero* by Theodore Maynard (New York: Macmillan, 1947).

All the World's a Stage *by Walter Hazen*

The actors, Richard Throckmorton and Thomas Stuart, are fictional characters. The information they give about Shakespeare and his theater is factually accurate. An authoritative source of information about Shakespeare is the "General Introduction" provided by David Bevington in his edition of *The Complete Works of Shakespeare, Updated Fourth Edition* (Longman, 1997). Another source is *Shakespeare's Theater* by Jacqueline Morley and John James (New York: Peter Bedrick Books, 1994).

Artemisia Gentileschi *by Barbara Littman*

All the people in this story are historical figures. The information about Artemisia Gentileschi and the art world of the Renaissance is factually accurate. Sources include *Artemisia Gentileschi, The Image of the Female Hero in Italian Baroque Art* by Mary D. Garrard (Princeton, NJ: Princeton University Press, 1989) and *The Italian Followers of Caravaggio* by Alfred Moir (Cambridge, MA: Harvard University Press, 1967).

Silk Road from China *by Judith Lloyd Yero*

Song Chau, the narrator, is a fictional character. The experiences he describes are based on descriptions told by those who traveled the early Silk Road. An excellent source of historical details about the Silk Road is *Life Along the Silk Road* by Susan Whitfield (Berkeley, CA: University of California Press, 2000).

The Daring Portuguese *by Lynnette Brent*

The sailor who narrates this story is a fictional character. The activities of Prince Henry's hired sailors are described in many historical documents. The events described in the story are based on accounts of those who survived the sea voyages on the African coast. *Prince Henry "The Navigator": A Life* by Peter Russell (New Haven: Yale University Press, 2000) describes the men, their goals, and their adventures.

Voyage Around the World *by Marianne McComb*

All the characters in this story are historical figures and the information is factually accurate. Sources include *Ferdinand Magellan* by Hawthorne Daniel (Garden City, NY: Doubleday, 1964) and *Magellan's Voyage Around the World: Three Contemporary Accounts by Antonio Pigafetta, Maximilian of Transylvania, and Gaspar Corrêa* (Evanston, IL: Northwestern University Press, 1962).

The Dragon and the Spanish Armada *by Sharon Franklin*

The English mother and her son Edwin are fictional characters. Sir Francis Drake, Queen Elizabeth I of England, Philip II of Spain, and Admiral Howard are historical figures. The details of the story about the defeat of the Spanish Armada are historically accurate. Sources include *The Campaign of the Spanish Armada* by Peter Kemp (New York: Facts On File Publications, 1988) and *The Spanish Armadas* by Winston Graham (Garden City, NY: Doubleday & Company, 1972).

Glossary of People and Terms to Know

alliance (uh•LY•uhns)—formal agreement or treaty between two or more nations to cooperate for specific purposes.

annul (uh•NUL)—cancel formally. In the Catholic Church, to annul a marriage means it never existed.

apprentice—person who worked under a skilled craftsman and learned his trade.

art patrons—wealthy people who supported artists by commissioning (ordering or buying) works from them.

As You Like It—comedy by William Shakespeare, first performed in 1599–1600.

auto da fé (AH•toh duh•FAY)—public meeting to announce the sentences of people found guilty by the Inquisition.

Baroque (buh•ROHK)—style in art and architecture in Europe from about 1550 to 1700. Baroque painting stressed realism, movement, and emotion. Baroque painters used real people as models. Bright colors and intense shadows gave drama to their paintings.

Boccaccio (boh•KAH•chee•OH), **Giovanni**—(1313–1375) Italian writer, author of the *Decameron*.

Borgia (BAWR•juh), **Cesare**—(1476–1507) Italian ruler, soldier, and politician; son of the man who became Pope Alexander VI. The ruthless Cesare became a cardinal at 18 and may have had his own brother killed.

bowls—popular game in England since the 1100s, played on a lawn, or "green." Lopsided balls called bowls are rolled at a smaller target ball.

broadsides—large sheets of paper printed on one side and used as news bulletins. Broadsides were posted in towns to tell people about important events.

Buddha (BOO•duh)—(563–483 B.C.) Indian philosopher and founder of Buddhism. His real name was Siddhartha Gautama. Buddha means "Enlightened One."

calligraphy (kuh•LIHG•ruh•fee)—beautiful handwriting, often involving curls and other small lines, which was frequently used in manuscripts copied by monks.

Cape Bojador (BOH•ha•DOHR)—point of land on Africa's west coast, just south of the Canary Islands. *Bojador* means "bulging cape" in Portuguese.

Caravaggio (kar•uh•VAH•joh), **Michelangelo**—(1571–1610) Italian painter who had a strong influence on Baroque painting.

caravan—group of travelers or traders traveling cross-country with pack animals.

caravel—small ship with three masts and lateen sails.

Castiglione (KAH•stihl•YOH•nay), **Baldassare** —(1478–1529) Italian courtier and man of letters. Castiglione's *Book of the Courtier* was published in 1528.

Charles V—(1500–1558) greatest of the Hapsburg emperors. He ruled over a vast empire that included Belgium, the Netherlands, Austria, Spain, and the Spanish lands in the Americas.

circumnavigated—completely circled.

city-state—independent, self-governing city and the territory around it.

coronation—ceremony in which a ruler is crowned.

courtier (KAWR•tee•uhr)—noble person in attendance at a royal court.

courtly love—idealized form of love popular in the courts of the Middle Ages and Renaissance. In courtly love, a knight or courtier devoted himself to a noble woman, who usually was married.

Decameron (duh•KAM•uhr•uhn)—collection of 100 tales by Boccaccio. The title, which means "ten days," refers to the time spent by Boccaccio's fictional young people in storytelling.

diplomat—person appointed to represent a government to other governments.

dissect—to divide into parts for study.

Drake, Sir Francis—(c. 1540–1596) English admiral and naval hero who circumnavigated the world and defeated the Spanish Armada.

dynasty—succession of rulers who belong to the same family.

eclipse—as an observer sees it, the darkening of one heavenly body, like the moon, by the shadow of another.

Edward—(1537–1553) king Edward VI of England, son of Henry VIII and his third wife, Jane Seymour. He became king in 1547.

Elizabeth—Elizabeth I (1533–1603), queen of England who ruled from 1558 to 1603. Elizabeth was the daughter of King Henry VIII and Anne Boleyn. Her reign was one of England's greatest periods.

English Channel—arm of the Atlantic Ocean between western France and southern England. The English Channel opens into the North Sea.

expedition—important journey by a group of people taken for a specific purpose.

falcon—bird with a short, curved beak and long, pointed wings. In the Middle Ages and Renaissance, falcons were trained to hunt game.

Ferdinand—Ferdinand II (1452–1516), king of Aragón (1479–1516). His marriage to Queen Isabella of Castile allowed them to work successfully toward a united, strong Spain.

fireships—English merchant ships that were purposely set on fire and sailed directly into Spanish ships.

flogged—whipped severely. A flogging was a common form of discipline used to control sailors and to punish criminals.

Galileo (gal•uh•LAY•oh)—(1564–1642) Galileo Galilei, Italian astronomer, mathematician, and physicist. His work formed the foundation of modern experimental science.

Gentileschi, Artemisia (JEHN•tee•LEHS•kee, ahr•tuh•MEE•zhuh)—(1593–c. 1653) Italian painter. Gentileschi was one of the followers of the famous painter Caravaggio.

Globe—famous London theater where William Shakespeare's plays were performed after 1599. The Globe was pulled down in 1644, after the Puritans closed the theaters. Restoration of the Globe began in 1987.

Golden Hind—only ship of Sir Francis Drake's fleet that survived to successfully circumnavigate the world in 1577–1580.

guild (gihld)—association of people in the same trade. Guilds set standards for the quality of their work, described the training by which an apprentice could become a full member, and protected businesses from outside competition.

Gutenberg (GOOT•uhn•BURG), **Johann**—(c. 1390–1468) German craftsman and inventor who invented a way of printing with movable type. Gutenberg's printing press was one of the most important inventions in world history.

Hamlet—famous tragedy by Shakespeare in which a Danish prince is urged by the ghost of his murdered father to get revenge.

Henry VIII—(1491–1547) king of England (1509–1547).

Henry, Prince—(1394–1460) called Prince Henry the Navigator, younger brother of Portugal's king. Prince Henry's school for navigators at Sagres near Cape St. Vincent was a center for mapmaking and shipbuilding. The prince sponsored many voyages of discovery.

heretics (HEHR•ih•tihks)—people accused of heresy, that is, of believing things that went against the teachings of the Catholic Church.

Howard—(1536–1624) Charles Howard, first earl of Nottingham. Lord Howard was lord high admiral of the English fleet that fought the Spanish Armada.

inlet—small or narrow body of water, like a bay or a cove.

Inquisition—from 1478 to 1808, formal investigation by representatives of the Roman Catholic Church into people's beliefs. Its goal was to find heretics and get rid of heresy. The Spanish government used the Inquisition to get rid of political enemies and as a way to control by terror.

Isabella—Isabella I (1451–1504), ruler of the Spanish states of Castile and León (1474–1504). Her marriage to King Ferdinand II of Aragón helped to unify Spain.

James I—(1566–1625) king of England (1603–1625). James I was the first Stuart king of England and the first to rule both England and Scotland. He became king upon the death of Elizabeth I.

jousts—combats between two knights using lances.

Julius Caesar—tragedy by William Shakespeare, first performed in 1599–1600.

Kublai Khan (KOO•bly KAHN)—(1215–1294) Mongol emperor of China, which had been conquered by his grandfather, Genghis Khan. Kublai Khan built his capital at Cambuluc, near today's Beijing.

Lapulapu—(c. 1490–c. 1560) Filipino chieftain now considered a national hero because he prevented the first European invasion of the Philippines.

lord chancellor—high official in England's government, the presiding officer in the House of Lords. Parliament is made up of the House of Lords (nobles and high-ranking church officials) and the House of Commons (common people).

lute—musical instrument like a guitar.

Macbeth—tragedy by William Shakespeare in which a Scottish nobleman decides to murder his king because three witches say he will be the next king.

Machiavelli (MAHK•ee•uh•VEHL•ee), **Niccolò**—(1469–1527) Italian diplomat, political writer, and historian. Machiavelli is considered the founder of modern political science.

Magellan, Ferdinand—(1480–1521) Portuguese sailor and navigator, leader of the expedition that was the first to travel completely around the globe.

Mary—(1516–1558) Mary I became queen of England in 1553. She was known as "Bloody Mary" because she had hundreds of Protestants executed in an attempt to restore the Catholic Church in England.

Mass—central service of worship in the Roman Catholic Church.

Medici (MEHD•ih•chee), **Lorenzo de'**—(1449–1492) Italian ruler, poet, and patron of the arts, known as "Lorenzo the Magnificent." A member of a great Italian banking family, Lorenzo ruled Florence from 1469 to 1492. He supported such artists as Leonardo da Vinci and Michelangelo.

Michelangelo (mih•kuhl•AN•juh•LOH)—(1475–1564) Italian artist, one of the greatest artists in world history. Among his works are the paintings in the Sistine Chapel in Rome and statues of David and Moses.

Midsummer Night's Dream, A—famous comedy by William Shakespeare. *A Midsummer Night's Dream* is about two pairs of mismatched lovers. It was first performed during the 1595–1596 season.

Moluccas (muh•LUHK•uhz) **Islands**—name for the Spice Islands, a group of islands in eastern Indonesia.

monastery (MAHN•uh•STEHR•ee)—home for monks, men who take vows to devote their lives to the religion and to live, work, and pray together.

More, Sir Thomas—(1478–1535) English statesman, author of *Utopia*, Catholic martyr, and saint.

Muslims—believers in Islam, a religion founded by the prophet Muhammad.

mutiny (MYOO•tin•ee)—revolt of a ship's crew against their captain.

navigation—planning, recording, and controlling the course of a ship. A person who does this work is called a navigator.

novice (NAHV•ihs)—person who has entered a religious order but has not yet taken final vows.

oasis (oh•AY•sis)—fertile or green spot in a desert or wasteland.

papacy (PAY•puh•see)—Roman Catholic Church government headed by the pope.

parchment—paper-like material made from animal skins that was often used in the preparation of books during the Middle Ages and the Renaissance.

Parr, Catherine—(1512–1548) sixth and last wife of Henry VIII of England. Theirs was a loving relationship that lasted four years until his death.

peers—English noblemen known as "peers of the realm." They hold government office in England's Parliament, in the House of Lords.

perspective—in painting, the use of lines and shading to give the impression of three dimensions on a flat, or two-dimensional surface.

Philip II—(1527–1598) king of Spain who reigned from 1556 to 1598. He was the strongest ruler in Europe at the time.

plague (playg)—highly infectious, widespread disease. In the 1300s, the bubonic plague, called the Black Death, killed one-third of Europe's population and about 65 million people worldwide.

Polo, Marco—(1254–1324) Italian merchant and traveler from Venice. When in his teens, Marco Polo traveled along the Silk Road to Asia with his merchant father. He spent many years with the Mongol emperor of China, Kublai Kahn, and then returned to Europe and wrote about his travels.

Porto Santo—one of the Madeira Islands.

Prince, The—famous and influential book by Machiavelli. It was written in 1513 and published in 1532.

psalm (sahlm) **book**—book containing the Psalms, a group of 150 sacred songs and poems that makes up a book of the Bible.

Puritans—members of a group in the Church of England during the 1500s and 1600s who wanted simpler worship and stricter morals.

rabbi (RAB•eye)—person trained in Jewish law, ritual, and traditions; Jewish religious leader.

Renaissance man—one who has broad intellectual interests and is well versed in both the arts and the sciences.

Revenge—Sir Francis Drake's flagship. A flagship carries the fleet commander and displays his flag.

Richard III—(1452–1485) English king believed to have had two young princes murdered in order to gain the throne. Shakespeare portrayed him as an evil hunchback in *Richard III*.

scaffold (SKAF•uhld)—platform that is used in the execution of condemned prisoners. It is where the noose or chopping block is placed.

Sforza (SFAWRT•suh), **Ludovico** —(1452–1508) powerful Italian prince. Sforza's court at Milan was one of the most splendid in Europe.

Shakespeare, William— (1564–1616) English poet, playwright, and actor considered by many to be the greatest dramatist of all time.

Silk Road—system of ancient caravan routes across Central Asia, along which traders carried silk and other goods.

South Sea—former name for the Pacific Ocean.

Spanish Armada (ahr•MAH•duh)—King Philip II's fleet of warships. The Spanish Armada consisted of 130 ships, 8,000 sailors, and 19,000 soldiers. The English defeated them in 1588.

strait—narrow channel that connects two bodies of water.

subjects—people who are under the rule of a government leader, such as a king or a queen.

Tang—dynasty in China that ruled from 681 to 907.

Thames (tems)—river in southern England that flows through London.

Torquemada, Tomás de
(TAWR•kuh•MAH•duh)—(1420–1498)
Grand Inquisitor of Castile and
Aragón in Spain from 1483 to 1498.
He used torture to identify
heretics and made the Inquisition
much harsher than it had been.

tournaments—contests in which
two groups of knights fight each
other on horseback, using lances
or swords or other weapons.

Tower of London—famous
prison in London, England.

treason—high crime of betraying
one's country.

Turkic lands—general term
for lands to the east of the
Caspian Sea, inhabited by peoples
speaking one of the Turkic family
of languages.

Twelfth Night—one of
Shakespeare's most famous comedies. *Twelfth Night* is about a girl
who disguises herself as boy and
becomes the servant of a duke
with whom she falls in love. It was
first performed in 1601–1602.

Utopia—Sir Thomas More's
literary masterpiece (1516) in
which he describes an ideal society.
More's book, written in Latin, was
widely translated and became very
popular throughout Europe.

vanishing points—points at
which parallel lines drawn in
perspective seem to meet.

verdict—judgment, or opinion,
about guilt or innocence in a trial.

Verrocchio (vuh•ROH•kee•oh),
Andrea del—(1435–1488)
Florentine sculptor and painter.
His most important works are
church decorations, statues, and
figure and portrait sculpture.

Vinci (VIN•chee), **Leonardo da**
—(1452–1519) Florentine artist,
scientist, and inventor.

Xuan Huang (SHOO•wen
HWANG)—Chinese Buddhist
monk who traveled the Silk Road
from 629 to 644. He brought
back Buddhist scriptures from
India and spent the rest of his life
translating them.

Acknowledgements

10 Alinari/Art Resource, NY.
12 Scala/Art Resource, NY.
15 © The Granger Collection.
19 North Wind Pictures Archives.
23 © Hulton-Deutsch Collection/ Corbis.
30 © Alinari/Art Resource, NY.
32, 34 © Stock Montage.
42 Hulton-Getty Picture Library.
46 © Art Resource, NY.
50 © Stock Montage.
53 © Superstock.
59, 67, 71 © Hulton-Getty Picture Library.
77, 80 © 1998 North Wind Pictures.
83 The Granger Collection.
88 © SuperStock.
94 © The Granger Collection
96 © Alinari/Art Resource, NY.
103, 105, 107 Hulton-Getty Picture Library.

113 © Stock Montage.
118 ©1998 North Wind Pictures.
126 from *The Complete Works of Shakespeare*, edited by David Bevington. Copyright 1997 by Addison-Wesley Educational Publishers Inc. Reprinted by permission.
128 © 1998 North Wind Pictures.
130 © The Granger Collection.
134 © Scala/Art Resource, NY.
137 © Stock Montage.
141, 149 The Granger Collection.
151 © Hulton-Getty Picture Library.
159 © 1994 North Wind Pictures.
160 © Hulton-Getty Picture Library.
162 © The Granger Collection.
167 © Gianni Dagli Orti/Corbis.
172, 175 © Hulton-Getty Picture Library.